PERSONAL PILGRIMAGE at MIDLIFE

One Day Soul Journeys for a Time of Transition

Also by Viki Hurst

Personal Pilgrimage: One Day Soul Journeys for Busy People

Viki Hurst

PERSONAL PILGRIMAGE at MIDLIFE

One Day Soul Journeys for a Time of Transition

Northstone

Editor: Michael Schwartzentruber
Design: Margaret Kyle
Proofreading: Dianne Greenslade
Cover photograph: Doug Menuez, PhotoDisc. Calligraphic background: Don Bishop, Artville.
Credits: Unless otherwise noted, source for selected quotations: the Internet

Northstone Publishing acknowledges the financial support of the Government of Canada, through the Book Publishing Industry Development Program, for its publishing activities.

Northstone Publishing is an imprint of Wood Lake Books Inc., an employee-owned company, and is committed to caring for the environment and all creation. Northstone recycles, reuses, and encourages readers to do the same. Resources are printed on recycled paper and more environmentally friendly groundwood papers (newsprint), whenever possible. The trees used are replaced through donations to the Scoutrees for Canada program. A percentage of all profit is donated to charitable organizations.

Canadian Cataloguing in Publication Data
Hurst, Viki, 1947 -
Personal pilgrimage at midlife
Includes bibliographical references.
ISBN 1-896836-45-3
1. Middle age persons – Religious life. 2. Pilgrims and pilgrimages. I. Title.
BL619.P5H872 2002 291.4'4 C2001-911642-X

Copyright © 2002 Viki Hurst
All rights reserved. No part of this publication may be reproduced – except in the case of brief quotations embodied in critical articles and reviews – stored in an electronic retrieval system, or transmitted in any form or by any means; electronic, mechanical, photocopying, recording, or otherwise, without prior written consent of the publisher or copyright holder.

Published by Northstone Publishing
an imprint of Wood Lake Books Inc., Kelowna, BC Canada

Printing 10 9 8 7 6 5 4 3 2 1

Printed in Canada
Transcontinental Printing

Dedication

To my best friend, Becky.

Contents

PART 3

Index of Inspirational Guides

Acknowledgments

I want to thank Northstone Publishing for its enthusiastic support of *Personal Pilgrimage*, and for the contributions this publisher makes to a better world. In particular, I want to thank my editor, Mike, and the designer of this book, Margaret, for their artful contributions to the quality of my work, and for their genuine enthusiasm whenever I turn over a manuscript to them for their final touch.

PART 1

PERSONAL PILGRIMAGE at MIDLIFE

Journeys to Midlife Balance

1

Journeys to Midlife Balance

I've walked the paths of the Torrey Pines Reserve many times since moving to San Diego about 13 years ago. My favorite path starts at the southern perimeter of the reserve, bordering the Torrey Pines golf course and driving range, but slowly leading me out of civilization and into a place with ancient history and unique flora. No trees line this particular trail – it is like walking into a desert wilderness. Lined with chaparral and other scrub brush, this path speaks of simplicity – for at least 20 minutes, there is no hint of the spectacular view about to unfold. The Torrey Pines hiking trails parallel the bluff edge that rises high above the Pacific Ocean. This is where I am headed. A certain bench awaits me – one where I have often found rest…and sometimes answers.

For a pilgrim like myself, this bench is as sacred a place as the waters of Lourdes, France – as healing, and as powerful. Sitting here with my journal, my bottle of water, and my daypack (which I affectionately refer to as my pilgrim's satchel), all of my senses point to the power that keeps the universe running. I feel the brisk wind that blows inland from the sea below. Quiet enfolds this place, except for the call of an occasional bird. Miles of unspoiled beaches stretch below me, and acres of tree-studded land in the distance. I'm sitting in the middle of one of the busiest cities in the world, and yet I am contained within one of the wildest stretches of land on the Southern California coast, not far from five-lane freeways, and yet not a car in sight.

The projects and deadlines that await me at home become less important as I take in the grandeur of this particular reality. I know that I contribute to the great turnings and churnings of the world, but this indescribable beauty would continue to exist, even if I failed to make that one important phone call in the morning. I am not in charge. What a relief.

Dozens of people pass by my bench. Some may be pilgrims, like myself, in search of enlightenment, or perhaps healing, receptive to a mystical experience of some sort. Others may simply be hikers, those who enjoy the very act of putting one foot in front of the other, in search of nothing but the exhilaration of being outdoors. Still others are meanderers, out to enjoy what San Diego has to offer in the way of natural beauty – they're not wearing hiking boots and they're not counting the miles.

Because I think of this place, and especially this bench, as a powerful, sacred site, I come here as a pilgrim today. Though it is simply a collection of narrow wooden slats screwed to wrought iron legs, the bench lifts me above the surface of the earth and projects my senses over the green-black ocean on the horizon and the pine trees in the distance, in a way that makes me not only one with the bench, but with the entire landscape. I feel somewhat related to the rare pine tree for which this reserve is named. These elegant trees suffer from persistent drought. Their roots are growing in difficult, sandy soil. They bear both scalding sun and blasting storms. Yet the trees continue to thrive, despite their hard times. I am like them. And so are many of us.

It is this mystical awareness that makes my experience and this bench sacred, and it's what makes me a pilgrim on this particular sunny day. I reach into my satchel and pull out a smooth, white rock, about the size of a dime, and I look around for someplace to put it. I picked up this stone while visiting the Puget Sound in the great Northwest, during a particularly adventurous Outward Bound trip several years ago. I place it beneath the bench – it is *for* the bench. A gift. A connection.

I come to this bench exploring questions about my life's mission and whether it's time to update my career map. Stress called me here. Feeling tired and spent for days on end, I needed to put aside my brilliant ideas and huge ambitions and put things in perspective. The night before this soul journey, I journaled about where I am in my life. As I wrote, most of the loose ends and questions that arose, even the wounds, pointed to career issues. Five years ago, as I entered what Gail Sheehy refers to as the "Second Adulthood," I made some big decisions about what to do with the second half of my life regarding my life's work. But have I taken the right path? I love all the things I do – teaching, coaching, training, consulting, writing – but to be fulfilled, do I have to do them *all?* My life is full, but is it *too* full? I seem so busy and sometimes so frantic, it's hard to squeeze in time for my aging mother, my other family members, my friends, my social life, my physical fitness program, my soul work. My writing told me that clearly it was time to take stock of my career and to make it the focal point of the next day's soul journey.

And so it is. With the quiet clamor of a few nearby birds and the subtle rustle of wind in my hair, new insights grace the journal page in front of me, and I realize it may indeed be time to update some of my old ideas about success and what it means to me. And then more questions: Should I downsize? Should I relocate? Should I try something different? And while change is a frightening prospect, I realize that the universe, as it displays itself in front of me in this very moment, is itself always changing. And yet it is the same. This sacred earth on which I live, and my own sacred sites, support my quest and are always available to me for peace and encouragement during times of fear, prosperity, joy, or change…if I take the time to visit.

While career is an important aspect of my life, at midlife there seem to be more things than ever to reflect upon, but few opportunities for doing so. There are times when I feel as if the dreams I had for my life have grown stale…times when I wonder if I have really contributed anything of value to my family and friends…times when I want to celebrate the wonder of my life…times when I question whether my relationships are genuine and times when I want to marvel at them…times when I wonder if I will ever get over some of the character defects that plague me and get in the way of my ability to grow…times when I want to achieve more, times when I want to redefine success, and times when I want to forget about it. But there is little time, it seems, to contemplate these important doubts and questions. I am one of those busy people for whom I wrote my first book – *Personal Pilgrimage: One Day Soul Journeys for Busy People* – but I somehow feel it is more critical than ever for me to put aside the roles of professor, personal coach, devoted daughter, available mom, businesswoman, good friend, cat owner, mentor…and make time to seek the deeper roles I might be asked to play within the deeper realities life has to offer.

Why is it more important than ever for me to seek deeper realities than the realities right in front of me? Three reasons.

First, at midlife, I feel that more is expected of me in the way of wisdom. My friends, family, students and clients expect me to have my life relatively all together, to know what's best, and to offer guidance. They call upon me for advice and support, and they expect me to be there for them. I don't think it's an unreasonable expectation. I expect it of myself. If a good and just society unfolds from the human heart, as I believe it does, then it's critical that I visit my heart and discover what is there, for I believe that there is where my wisdom resides. Wisdom is not necessarily having all the right answers. As I've often heard it said, wisdom is having all the right questions. It's having a perspective on your experiences, born of reflection, and the willingness to share your perspective in an offering of love and compassion. After 50-plus years of living, I want to have plenty of perspective to share. And personally, I believe the world can use all the wisdom we midlifers can muster.

The *second* reason it's more important than ever for me to be a seeker today: I won't be here forever. I can't say that I am completely convinced that someday I will die, but with the deaths of several family members and friends over the past few years, I've seen what that looks like and I strongly suspect that it will also happen to me. The old saying *life is short* is true, and I want to live it not only productively, but also in ways that are meaningful during the rest of my stay.

Information is power, silence is golden

We've often heard that *information is power*. And that's especially true today in the Information Age. But for me, the flip side of that maxim is *silence is golden*. Both together represent balance.

Information keeps us up-to-date and competitive. It keeps us stimulated and alive. In her groundbreaking book *Leadership and the New Science,* Margaret Wheatley asserts that in organizations, information is our best ally; it's what keeps the lifeblood flowing through an organization's veins.

Without information, we are in the dark. Information doesn't have to be written or even spoken. It's a mysterious building element of the universe's energy bank. From information comes wisdom.

On the other hand, information is killing us. In a recent study conducted by Reuters, entitled *Dying for Information,* managers and executives from all over the world reported that information overload was interfering with the ability to make

And the *third* reason I am a seeker today is because my health depends upon it. As I grow older, my ability to withstand stress has diminished somewhat, and I must, at times, put aside the flurry of activity that gives me so much fulfillment, and seek balance. While I sometimes hate to admit that I have reached the age where slowing down is a must, my body, mind, and soul insist. I have to heed the call to balance or suffer the consequences of illness, fatigue, and impatience. Those things come quicker than ever when I ignore the signs that point to a time-out.

For me, time-outs often take the form of soul journeys like the ones I take to Torrey Pines. These mini-pilgrimages, or *personal pilgrimages* as I like to call them, parallel the practice of the traditional pilgrimage, and the four phases of these journeys help me stay focused. As I would for any trip, I put my personal pilgrimages on my calendar, so that they are intentional and planned. Though I only take them occasionally – maybe five or six times a year – they have become the mainstay of my spiritual fitness program, and I believe they will help sustain me through these midlife years. I recommend them heartily to my friends, family members, clients, and readers of all ages, but especially to those of us who are entering or are in the midst of our middle years. Here's to our quest for wisdom, peace and balance, and our willingness to share it.

timely decisions, with family life and health. David Shenk, in his book *Data Smog,* asserts that the information highway is full of a new kind of pollution: data crud. His book shows that information in truckloads can be a nuisance, rather than a blessing.

To counteract the debilitating effects of information overload, I maintain that silence is the perfect antidote. Downloading the mind files from time to time to allow your brain to breathe and rest is critical to maintaining high brain functioning. How can we do that when we are so busy?

Many workplaces are setting aside space for silence. Ten minutes a day with no phones. Quiet zones. Meditation rooms. If you work in a place like that, take time out and use the space to get clear. Re-energize with silence. If you don't work in a place that honors spaces of silence, find some space yourself. Go there for lunch or for a ten-minute break. Don't talk. Don't write. Don't think. Listen only to your breathing. Then come back to your desk, your work, your life, refreshed and ready to go.

Space your weeks and months with times for silence, as well. Take personal pilgrimages for whole days of silence, or take long, luxurious baths for just a few moments of peace and quiet.

The gentle turn

Midlife, as most of us know, is not necessarily a matter of chronology. It's not just about how many years we've spent on the planet. The lifespan for human beings has not changed significantly for thousands of years and remains at about 120 years. At the same time, life *expectancy* has changed some. Most experts say the average life expectancy for a female today is 72 years; for a male it's 68 years. So is midlife at 60 – based on lifespan? Or is midlife at 34–36, based on life expectancy? I know that for myself midlife gets further and further away every few years. In my 20s, I expected midlife to arrive somewhere around age 35. In my 30s, midlife was about 45. Today, in my 50s, I realize I am at the midlife mark, but that mark still seems to be out there somewhere beyond my current age. Maybe midlife is at 58? 62?

Midlife isn't so much about age, then. It's about the accelerating physical and mental changes that occur, as they do in most people, from the ages of about 45 to 65. At some point within that period, we may feel like completely different people than we were just three to five years before. Mental, emotional, and physical changes, all accelerating at once, can wreak havoc with our lives. While many writers note the spectacular transformations that occur in people at midlife, the term *midlife crisis* is still used to describe the almost inevitable havoc.

There are many analogies and labels for this time of life. In her recent book *New Passages*, Gail Sheehy puts midlife at about age 45 and calls this age *middlescence* – the beginning of a "second adulthood." Author John C. Robinson likes to think of life in terms of seasons and in his book *Death of a Hero, Birth of the Soul,* he refers to midlife for men as the transition between summer and fall. In Carole Hyatt's book on how to plan a new strategy for midlife, she calls the process *Shifting Gears.* The great psychiatrist Carl Jung referred to the middle years as "the afternoon of life."

Because I like to think of life as a journey, I sometimes refer to midlife as a gentle turn in the road – not a crossroads, though as we make the turn we may immediately encounter a crossroad or two, but a turn we must inevitably take as we make our ultimate pilgrimage. As we make the turn, we do it gently, because we stop hurrying quite so much. In fact, we may feel a bit tired out from our journey thus far. Or we may feel more energized than ever. Either way, to sustain ourselves through the remaining journey, we must be vital, healthy, and aware. That may mean repacking our pilgrim's "satchel" with new sustenance in the form of new ideas, new behaviors, and new priorities.

At this time in our lives, many of us make physical health a new priority, in order to improve the quality of our journey. We make time to discover new vitamins, get regular checkups, find new herbal remedies to enhance memory and physical vigor. We exercise more and we rest more. We watch what we eat and we learn how to cope with the inevitable physical discomforts that come with aging.

But while many of the changes we undergo as we make the gentle turn are physical, some of the most challenging are spiritual, according to many midlife experts. The main reason for the change in our spiritual perspective is that at this stage of our lives many of us are coming face to face with mortality. We feel the inevitability of physical deterioration in our own aching muscles and creaking bones. Family members and friends experience serious illnesses, even death. This encounter with mortality urges us to take stock of our lives and explore its larger meaning

So just as we have learned to take advantage of the miracles of health science, so we must learn to experience the miraculous healing and wisdom that comes from spiritual engagement. Engaging the spirit means communing with that part of ourselves that lies deep within, so that it can help point us toward the meaning in our worldly activities and physical relationships. Most writers about midlife place a great deal of emphasis on this idea of meaning and the role it plays in the second half of our lives. Sheehy says, "the search for meaning in whatever we do becomes the universal preoccupation of Second Adulthood."

Sheehy refers to this search for meaning as "the feeding and crafting of the soul," and she says it is "the real work of one's Second Adulthood." In fact, many writers call the search for meaning our *soul work.*

Notice the use of the word *work.* We don't take a sports car down this path; we traverse it with feet of clay, one foot in front of the other, uphill and down. And if we are smart, we map and re-map. We find tools and practices that will help us stay on the path. If we thought midlife was going to be a time to cruise through life, many of us are going to be surprised. To find meaning, we have to truly search, and sometimes in places we might never have expected.

For many midlifers, the search is taking place within the context of renewed commitments to formal religion. Two of my own friends recently went back to the Catholic Church they openly renounced throughout their young adult years. "I never realized how much I missed the ritual and the ceremony of the church," says John, whose adult daughter took him to Mass whenever he visited with her and her family. "It seemed silly to hold on to old rebellions against authority when my soul was crying out for structure and tradition. I decided I had outgrown the need to be right and wanted, instead, to be fed." Others have adopted spiritual practices foreign to their younger years. My born-again Christian friend, Sherry, told me her mother would "roll over in her grave" if she knew Sherry was practicing Buddhist forms of meditation today. "I probably don't believe everything the Buddhists preach and I still think of myself as born-again," she told me, "but the meditation helps me with every aspect of my life and helps me feel healthier all the way around."

Like physical fitness, then, which requires us to take time for exercise, rest, and checkups, spiritual fitness requires us to set aside time as well – for church, for meditation, for journaling and storytelling, for connecting with others who share our quest for spiritual maturity. But while we may have imagined a midlife of more leisure and free time, an increasing number of us report that we are busier than ever, busier than we were in our youth, busier, even, than five years ago.

The postmodern midlifer

Postmodern: Up until now, I have heard of no better term to describe the age we live in, as it is juxtaposed to the modern age of predictable, linear, material movement through life. Science, which during the Age of Enlightenment closed the door on mystical views of the world, may have reopened the door to spirituality. With chaos and quantum theories pointing to the true mysteries of the universe, we have a different context for life – not necessarily a *new* context, for it is readily backed by ancient teachings about how life really is – unfathomable, impossible to completely analyze with the rational mind, and inseparable from our consciousness. We have been reintroduced to a universe we cannot control nor thoroughly understand, which should give us pause. While we may have thought we knew our place in the world, now we must rethink.

At the same time, we have moved into an age that requires us to be more competitive than ever to survive, faster than ever, and more global. We must think quicker and bigger. The reason we need to be swifter than ever is the advent of electronic communication. While there is so much meaning to be found in this postmodern age, we simply don't have time to look for it. Gail Sheehy puts it this way in *New Passages:*

> Everything – money, war, political change, the rise and fall of great corporations – moves faster while our attention spans grow shorter. Indeed, with our E-mail boxes and our fax and phone machines always "on," we have invaded our own solitude with an accelerated demand for immediate action and reaction. We seldom make time to process even the most meaningful experiences of our lives; we just speed through them.

My client Christen is a good example of this. Christen is one of those people who gathers awards like my bookshelves gather dust. She doesn't even try. Graphic design became her second career about seven years ago and she went after success with a vengeance. "I felt like I had to outrun my younger counterparts to keep up," she told me. To stay on top of graphics software and design trends, she read every slick consumer magazine and every graphic design trade journal that came across her desk. In addition, she visited scores of websites every day, just to be current. She worked long into many nights to design brilliant advertising layouts and corporate identity packages, neglecting every other aspect of her life.

"After the last awards dinner, where I won two trophies for a campaign we had done for one of our biggest clients, I went home and just started sobbing," she says. "I couldn't even tell if it was for joy or for what. I couldn't go to work the next day, I was so worn out." After a long talk with her husband, Michael, she realized that she hated the latest round of trophies. "They signified my exhaustion rather than my pride in my work," she told me. "I couldn't take pleasure in bringing them home and setting them up on my desk, because they didn't mean anything to me. I hid them in a closet."

I suggested that Christen take an entire week just to celebrate, turning off her computer, cell phone and fax machine, and throwing her Palm Pilot in a drawer. "Go to dinner, have friends over, have Michael bake you a cake," I said. "Do something wonderful for yourself every night." The weekend, I told her, was for exploring what these awards really did mean to her and whether they were important enough to keep burning the midnight oil for.

"But I don't have *time* to explore stuff like that!" she moaned.

Christen has to *make* time. At midlife, she may feel she has to move faster to keep up with her younger colleagues, but maturity calls upon us to find meaning in our work. The spontaneous crying she did the night after the awards ceremony was a call to balance, and balance sometimes means putting aside *outward* work and doing a little *inner* work. I often coach people to put aside a day for gardening or cooking. Just that. No phone calls. No e-mail. No faxes. Heed the *inner* call.

In addition to a world that calls for both wisdom and speed, today's midlifer faces a longer life expectancy than generations before. Some, like Christen, realize that retirement – stepping back from the workday world and letting go of work challenges – will not fulfill a remaining second half of life and they begin new vocations. In *Shifting Gears: Planning a New Strategy for Midlife,* author Carol Hyatt reports that for many people, longer life expectancy has given rise to the desire to live a fuller second half, with new careers as a focal point.

For many of us, a longer life not only means staying abreast of new technologies, keeping up with our younger colleagues, and acquiring new skills, it also means opening our minds to ideas we may have never before entertained. Absolute truths and strong opinions are called into doubt. "I never thought I would see the day when I would agree with my son about medications to relieve depression," my friend Bill told me. "He's been living with it all his life and my approach was 'Get out of bed, pull up your bootstraps and snap out of it!' The reading I've been doing recently about brain chemistry and the work researchers are doing to unlock the mysteries of the brain – I've changed my mind completely." We have to keep reading and remain open-minded as we move through our longer lives.

It's not just midlifers who are living longer as time rolls by. Our parents are living longer today, too. Almost everywhere I go, midlife men and women are escorting mom or dad to the grocery store, doctor appointments, on strolls through the neighborhood, and wherever else they need to go. My sister and I have made a commitment to our mother's quality of life. Living with the effects of a recent stroke and several other serious illnesses, Mom requires a great deal of time from both of us and we find ourselves coordinating many of our work and social obligations around her schedule. Most of my friends are in the same position. Some have even taken their mom or dad into their homes, resulting in major transitions not only for their parents, but for themselves as well.

In addition to our need or desire to work longer, harder, and faster; to take care of aging parents and our own health; to learn new skills and open our minds to new ideas; to read all our e-mail and answer all our phone messages; we are also called upon to impart wisdom. We have lived through war, participated in political protest, experienced intense generational schisms and global power shifts, taken part in hilarious fads, suffered the personal trauma of loss, and rejoiced in the triumph of personal success. What do we have to say about all of that? Sheehy, in *New Passages,* suggests that at this stage of our lives we have "responsibilities for mentoring the next generation and civilizing our communities, country and planet."

Given the postmodern age we live in, at midlife, the challenge of finding time to mentor a whole generation – not to mention the entire planet – seems mind-boggling. Talk about *work!* But if we don't do it, who will?

2

Midlife Issues for Healing & Enlightenment

Among the myriad issues midlifers are dealing with today, the 12 discussed in this chapter appear to be among the most pressing. Drawn from research, as well as from experience with my own colleagues, clients, students, family and friends, these concerns represent those most talked and written about, and perhaps those most in need of exploration, at midlife. These are the issues that require us to set aside time to do *inner work* so that we can find and impart meaning.

In the modern world of analytical science, finding answers was of paramount importance. We researched and explored in order to answer questions. Today, in the postmodern world, we are more willing to live with the chaos that represents the natural state of the universe. We are, as many Eastern philosophers say, willing to "live in the question." And so as we explore our lives at the midpoint, it is helpful to have the right questions for contemplation and meditation. We *may* discover answers to our questions. On the other hand, the questions may lead to more questions. Or unsought answers. In any event, the journey is as important as the destination, and the questions as important as the answers.

Career

Just because you have reached midlife does not mean you have to change careers. Many writers and researchers point to midlife as a time of upheaval, a time when we go off automatic pilot and suddenly begin to wonder if this is "all there is." For many of us, that means wondering if this is all there is to work and re-examining our career choices. But for many others, careers have been fulfilling and we are simply eager to pursue leisure activities, new hobbies, and new experiences. Work sometimes becomes a second priority at midlife, not because we are dissatisfied with work, but because it is time for something new.

Whether we change careers is not as important as *reflecting* on work, on what it means to us and on what it has meant over the years. Regardless of how we feel about our careers, midlife is a time to articulate our work philosophy, so that we can impart wisdom through our own life experiences. At midlife, even if we have changed careers once or twice, and even if we love the careers we are in now, a new motivation for work typically unfolds. The thrill of the first paycheck is far behind and the idea that we have to keep achieving in order to experience success may not be as appealing. Now we are being *called* – away from the mundane and toward the *meaningful.*

And how do we answer the call? With time and care – time to re-examine the true meaning of our careers and work choices, and with great care for our deepest selves. At midlife, this self-examination requires more than a résumé review. This time, we are not only taking stock of our skills, traits, and experience, we are taking stock of our deepest values, priorities, and desires.

My client Frank worked in the field of purchasing for 22 years, moving up the corporate ranks of several major manufacturing companies and achieving a high level of security and a long dreamed-of quality of life for his family. Suddenly, Frank found himself embroiled in some unpleasant corporate politics that tempted him to leave the company he had been with for 12 years. The stress of personality and value clashes brought Frank to the brink of quitting his job. But where would he go next?

"Day in and day out, it's always the same," he told me. "Everyone's out for themselves and the teamwork everyone keeps talking about is nothing but a bunch of individuals with their own agendas. My days consist of nothing but one meeting after another. They don't know how to get anything done without having some kind of meeting. It's a waste of time!"

Frank decided it might be time for a major change. He and I worked together to uncover some of his childhood dreams, what he liked to do best when he wasn't working, and how he would really like to spend the rest of his work life.

These are some of the questions I asked Frank to answer.

1. **What is work?** Some people describe their income-producing activities not as work, but as passion, or fun, or sheer joy. They say, "I don't think of what I do as *work*." What, then, is work? Do we have to do it? Why?

2. **What does it mean to be called?** Many people think of clergy, missionaries, and saints as being *called.* But an increasing number of career experts are referring to any career as a calling, regardless of content. How do we know when or if we have been called? Have you answered your calling?

3. **What had you learned about career by the time you were 8? 18? 28?** What have you learned about career, sum total, today?

4. **What did you like to do best when you were five years old?** Before we were told about careers, before we had to make critical work choices, we followed our true interests and passions. We scribbled joyfully not to make art but to experiment; we dug in the dirt not to landscape but to feel and smell the earth and to discover what was beneath it; we sang songs not to entertain but to express ourselves. Sometimes our true calling resides in our five-year-old selves.

5. **What do you think your purpose or mission is?** This particular question may take more time to review than the others, and perhaps more journaling, but if we consider all that has been put before us and all that has been given us in the way of resources, we may be able to articulate a mission statement for ourselves that will begin to be, and continue to be, our overarching guide to career – and life.

6. **What would you do with your life if money were no object?** Sometimes we connect work to money and security. If we disengage these parallels, do we

get a different perspective on work? If we were able to pursue only that which interested us, what would those interests be?

7. **How would you like your eulogy to read?** Few people say they want to be remembered for putting in 16-hour workdays or for meeting critical work deadlines. In fact, most people say they want to be remembered for their values or for the contributions they have made to family and friends. If we want to be remembered by those most important to us once we have gone, we may find that we would live our lives differently and that our careers or work methods would change.

8. **What advice would you give future generations about work and career?** If at midlife we have the wisdom the world needs, this question bears a great deal of thought. Think about how you were advised in your young adult years. Did you receive good advice? What advice do you wish you had received? Once you think about all you learned from your career and work experiences, you can formulate your personal work philosophy.

9. **Would you have done anything differently with your early career, if you knew what you know today?** Taking stock of our successes and failures can help us with the answer to this question. Once we see that our choices make up the life we live, we may find the courage we need to continue to make choices that will help us lead a fulfilling life.

10. **What do you need to do to make your life more fulfilling as you make "the gentle turn"?** An inventory of what is missing and what is fulfilling in our lives today will help us determine where to go from here. Life is short and now is the time to determine how to imbue it with the most value and meaning possible, although it is never too early nor too late for that. To make life more fulfilling, do we have to make new choices about work and career?

After a number of career assessments and a good deal of inner exploration, my client Frank determined that, for him, work provided the financial means for nurturing a healthy family. Ultimately, his career examination helped him determine that he was called to provide for his family in the best way possible. His career in purchasing was a means of providing wealth and security for his family and he had contributed a great deal to the success of the organizations for which he had worked.

Nevertheless, he also had a gnawing sense that something was missing and as he explored his childhood and what he truly enjoyed doing, he reconnected with his love of photography. He had received his first Kodak Brownie as a third-grader and had taken it with him on his Scouting activities throughout high school, becoming known as the troop photographer. He took photography classes in high school and was engrossed in the school's photography club. His photographs took on increasing technical sophistication throughout college, when he displayed some of them in competitions and shows. He loved photography and was good at it, but as he became more entrenched in his business degree, he replaced the time he spent on photography with work activities, professional associations, networking, and building the financial base for a family. He decided to ride out the inevitable political upheavals at his workplace in order to gain the benefits of a good job.

Frank wrote his mission statement like this: To capture life's beauty and grandeur for the enjoyment of others. He realized he could do this through his career – allowing his family to enjoy the beauty and grandeur of life through the security and affluence provided from the compensation he received for work – and he also realized he could capture the beauty and grandeur of life on film. He was called to be a father, uncle, grandfather, husband, *and* photographer. He was not called to be a purchasing professional, but his purchasing career had allowed him to achieve his ultimate mission.

Whether it's time to make a major career change or to determine how to make your current career more fulfilling, take time to reflect. Take stock of your skills, traits, and experience, but examine also your values, priorities, and mission. Ask yourself what it means to be successful. Determine if it's time to do something different. And share what you have learned.

Mortality

Most midlife experts agree that the primary reason for upheaval in the middle years is a *real* recognition that life ends. We've always known, intellectually, that life ends, but at midlife, as we begin to lose our parents, aging aunts and uncles, and our friends, we see what death really looks like and we begin to wonder how it will look on us.

Some ancient cultures depicted death not as a beast that snatches life away from us, but as a celebratory event that introduces us to the next one. In North America's youth-oriented culture, death is considered a failure and we do everything we can to keep from going there. Kathleen Brehony, in her book *Awakening at Midlife*, points out that more healthcare dollars are spent in the last six months of a person's life than in any previous years, just to stave off death. Fear and denial are natural reactions to the notion of death in Western cultures.

But "Death," wrote Carl Jung, "is a fearful piece of brutality; there is no pretending otherwise. It is brutal not only as a physical event, but far more so psychically... The actual experience of the cruelty and wantonness of death can so embitter us that we conclude there is no merciful God, no justice, and no kindness."

To stave off the bitterness that can come with the loss of a loved one, or the potential loss of our own selves, we must move from denial to acceptance – this was the profound conclusion of Elisabeth Kübler-Ross, which resulted from her studies on death and gave rise to the hospice movement.

Exploring the awesome subject of death and dying may seem a depressing prospect. On the other hand, such exploration can yield powerful insights that move us into a more invigorating second half of life. Knowing that we will die can push us to live life with more gusto. As Jung also pointed out, "death can appear as a joyful event. In the light of eternity it is a wedding...the soul attains, as it were, its missing half, it achieves a wholeness."

When my best friend Suzanne died from a form of intestinal cancer several years ago, I watched her deteriorate physically even as she blossomed spiritually. Even as she lost weight, hair, and the rosy luster of her skin, she began to glow almost as if a bright light were shining from within. Because there had been no known recovery from her form of cancer, she made the decision to forego aggressive treatment and accepted her destiny with complete grace. She continued to entertain in her home, even when she could not be present. We, her friends and family, sat in her living room and waited for the moments when she had the strength to see us. And when she did, she wanted to talk about us, about our lives and what we all meant to her.

On the last day I saw Suzanne, I read a portion of my first book to her, prior to its publication. When I looked up from that reading, she was beaming at me. "Good!" she said. "Good! Viki, do you know how far you have come since I first met you?" And she proceeded to outline my life in major milestones, letting me know that I had accomplished much in the eight years she had known me, and that I was someone she was proud to call a friend. I will always remember Suzanne as someone who cared very much about me, not as someone who was dying.

Suzanne's death brought to mind many questions. Exploring them has brought me comfort not only about her death, but an acceptance of what death can really be. The following are some of the questions I answered for myself shortly after her death. I suggest that these are good questions for finding midlife wisdom about mortality.

1. **What is death?** Not the dictionary definition. But what is death to you? A beast that snatches you away from life? Or an event that introduces you to the next one? This kind of exploration may require some reading and some frank discussions with others.

2. **Why do we fear death?** Thinking about the ways our families encountered and dealt with death, about the messages we have received from the popular media, and our culture orientation toward mortality, can reveal important insights about where our fear of death may come. If we had been raised differently, would we fear death?

3. **What will sustain you through death?** What will you need to go from here to there? For most people, a relationship with some Higher Power is important, as it affords a guide to the unknown. For others, friends and family are of primary importance. Pooling all our resources for managing stress will be critical. What are those resources?

4. **What had you learned about death by the time you were 8? 18? 28?**

5. **When we die, do our souls live on?** Facing death often means coming to grips with our spiritual beliefs. Whether we have souls; whether there is life after death and if so, in what form; whether we believe in God and if so, in what form;

these are important considerations as we draw to the close of life. These are also important considerations as we live our lives to the fullest.

6. **Are we in a constant decline toward death?** Western cultures embrace what is known as a "decline model" of life. This model states that from about the age of 20 we start a physical and mental decline that simply continues until we die. But there are many studies to refute this model. Some show that we continue to develop mentally and even physically even into our 70s. Understanding our belief about this model may require a bit of reading and research.

7. **Are you ready to die?** We never know how we would feel if we were told we had only a short time left to live. But if we imagine that to be the case today, what would our reaction be and what would we have to put in order?

8. **How have others who have died made an impact on your life?** Even if we don't believe in an afterlife, it's easy to see how people live on through the work and ideas they have contributed. Taking a quick inventory of the lives that have had the most impact on our own way of life can yield important discoveries about the meaning of both life and death.

9. **How are life and death alike?** What monumental meanings are embedded in both life and death?

10. **What do you need to do to accept your mortality?** There may be signs that we have not accepted mortality. How is our health? How are our relationships? If they are not good and we are living as if they are not important, we may not have accepted the fact that we are not going to be here forever to put things straight. If we are not ready to die today, we may need to ask ourselves what we need to do to get ready.

Before Suzanne died, she told me that, for her, death meant moving to another dimension and that she was eager to explore that dimension. In addition, I believe she focused lovingly on her friends and family before her death so that she could leave us with comfort and so that she could detach from the physical pain and discomfort that came from her particular form of cancer. As she was dying, she cared not only for us, but for herself. For me, Suzanne was the perfect model of both life and death.

Taking time to face death as a mere topic for exploration, loaded though it may be with psychic charge, can give us the insight and wisdom for living the second half of our lives with gusto and meaning. Sharing the answers we have discovered about mortality – with our friends, family, and loved ones – is an important midlife responsibility that could contribute to a changed consciousness about death and dying in our culture.

Sexual identity

Understanding our sexual identity – who we are as sexual beings – is critical to midlife wisdom. Sexual identity includes how we feel about sex, what role it plays in our lives, and what role we would *like* it to play in our lives. Understanding these things is to gain perspective on our whole selves, and on our picture of life itself.

To understand our sexual identity, we must ponder our very conception, because that is where sexual identity begins. At conception, we are genetically coded to be either male or female, and by the fifth week of pregnancy, we actually have either male or female genitals. That is part of our sexual identity. But only a small part.

Our full sexual identity is shaped by three main factors: *cultural underpinnings, personal history*, and *hormonal changes*. Taking a look at how all three of these factors have shaped our sexual identity will give us a good understanding about our sexual attitudes and behaviors today, how they have contributed to who we are, and how they may contribute to who we are becoming. For instance, we might reflect on how the following *cultural underpinnings* have shaped our sexual identity:

- religious tenets
- the depiction of sex in art and entertainment
- legal sanctions regarding sexual behavior and divorce
- gender roles
- economic trends
- ethnic background

These are but a few of the cultural areas that have profound effect on sexual identity. We must also consider *personal history*:

- family upbringing
- religious upbringing
- romance
- adults with whom we had relationships in childhood and adolescence
- friends, lovers and spouses, and their families

Finally, hormonal changes that cause alterations in health, appearance, and sex drive have a tremendous effect on how we identify as sexual beings.

While cultural underpinnings, personal history, and hormonal changes have a profound impact on shaping sexual identity, none of these are as important as our reflective capabilities. Exploring the meaning of sex in our lives yields important insights about who we are in relation to the rest of the world. Taking time to ponder the culture, history, and biology that have helped form sexual identity, and then articulating our values, our experience, our hopes, and our fears about sex and sexuality are invaluable midlife activities.

My friend Marilyn remarried about six years ago at the age of 50. She is delighted to report that from the very beginning of this marriage, she has experienced fully satisfying, delightful sex with her second husband. Because this is a drastic shift from the experience with her first husband, she's had a few questions to ask herself about this change of events. And so has her adult daughter, curious about her encounter with this newly glowing mom. The two have had several deep, meaningful discussions about sex over the past few years, answering questions similar to the ones below. Marilyn reports that the discussions have yielded new insights about herself physically, mentally, emotionally, and spiritually, and have helped her pass on information to her daughter in a way that was impossible when she was a younger mother without much experience. Here are some of the questions Marilyn and her daughter have discussed in recent years.

1. **What role has religion played in shaping your sexual identity?** Though religion does not play as widespread a role in shaping sexual attitudes as it did in centuries or even decades past, religious tenets learned from childhood

can continue to affect attitudes about sex for a lifetime. Exploring what was learned in childhood is valuable to determining sexual identity. Exploring religious tenets from current belief systems is also important.

2. **What roles have culture, personal history, and biology played in shaping your sexual identity?** In particular, thinking about the societal changes that have occurred in your lifetime can yield great insight about sexual identity.

3. **How would you describe your sexual identity? Find some adjectives.** While it may be important to think about how others perceive you as a sexual being, more important is to determine your own self-perception. Is it a perception that is appealing or disturbing or somewhere in between?

4. **What role do you want sex to play in your life today?** Many midlifers decide that sex will not take a prominent role at this time in their lives, based on a number of factors – difficulty in finding appropriate partners, diminished interest and sex drive, busy lifestyle. But many are simply victims to the biological and cultural changes taking place in their lives. They don't make active decisions. They say they don't have a choice. But deciding on the role of sex in your life is empowering, and I highly recommend it.

5. **What is sexy to you?** For many of us at midlife, arousal occurs when a partner or potential partner simply sits and listens attentively. We aren't looking for a chiseled chin or bulging muscles, big blue eyes or sexual prowess; we want authenticity, compassion, empathy, and gentleness. It may be useful, or at least enlightening, to know what turns you on.

6. **What do you value about sexual activity? What do you fear?** In our younger years, sex may have been a basis for self-esteem, for pleasure, and for fun. It was the way we built families and it was a way to learn, take risks, and have new adventures. We may derive the same benefits from sex today. We may have found new ones. On the other hand, we may have learned that sex can be a source of confusion and division. Being conscious of the benefits and drawbacks of sex can help us to understand our sexual identity and to develop a conscious sexual perspective.

7. **What had you learned about sex by the time you were 8? 18? 28?**

8. **How does your body perception affect your attitudes about sex?** By midlife, we may find that our organs are thickening, especially around the middle, our muscles have succumbed to the forces of gravity, our hair may be graying or thinning, our hearing and sight may be diminishing, our skin drying out, and our fat staying put. If so, how does this affect our sexual identity? Some midlifers, once they are aware of their own perceptions about their bodies, take better care of them. If your body awareness has been negative, you might gain a new awareness. Perhaps you can think of your body as an exquisite vessel for that wise and sacred spirit of yours.

9. **What advice do you have for future generations about sex?** Sex is sometimes a difficult teacher and we don't want to learn some of our toughest lessons in vain. One way to make sure our experience has value is to share it with others.

10. **If it weren't for sex...** How would you finish this sentence (besides with, "I wouldn't be here")?

One surprising outcome for Marilyn, which came from exploring her sexuality, was the realization that because she can truly change and *does* change, life has more to offer than she realized. New doors began to open in her career as she understood herself more, and family relationships began to improve. Instead of Marilyn the timid, passive one, Marilyn has become the empowered, assertive one, who deserves to relish every aspect of life. "So many possibilities!" she enthuses. "Maybe I'll even start to enjoy cooking some day!"

Body awareness

Since we can't rely on demographers, sociologists, or biologists to tell us exactly when we are going to reach midlife, because they all have different answers, how will we know? Is it possible that I was actually at midlife when I reached the age of 36, since, as a woman, I am expected to live to be about 72? That might mean that now, at the age of 50, I am actually into old age. But then, who knows? Long lifelines are features of both sides of my family, so if I live to be more than 100, maybe my midlife is actually right now, at this stage of my life, the 50s.

There may really be no such thing as midlife, if we look at our lives as circles rather than as linear lifelines. Where we begin and end could be just about anywhere on the circle, if we take our whole being into account. When does full consciousness arrive? At birth? Or at death?

These are philosophical questions we could discuss for years to come. But if we look at our midlife bodies in the here and now, one thing is certain: In most human beings, an array of changes seems to take place all at once between the ages of 45 and 65. They don't really happen overnight. They are gradual. However, many changes accelerate and intensify around this age, and for most of us, the acceleration and intensity tell us we are entering the second half of life.

Some consider these biological changes to be a downturn in the life cycle. There is a sense of loss – loss of youth, loss of beauty, loss of hopes and dreams. Others ignore the changes or try to hide them. Still others accept them, honor them, and go with them. There are many ways to deal with these changes psychologically. But these changes are real. And they are inevitable.

So what are these physical changes that define midlife?

Skin. Wrinkles, sags, and age spots may plague the skin at midlife, because the middle layer of skin thins and with it, the supply of protein fibers that give the skin its elasticity. Not only that, but sun exposure catches up with us in our 30s and 40s. By the same token, my friend Jacquelynn, a cosmetologist who knows just what to do for many of these changes in the skin, says she sees a certain glow in the skin of men and women who have a sense of humor about aging skin. "It's an indefinable thing, the way some people just have a glow about getting older, but it's beautiful to see," she insists. She says that with the loss of elasticity comes a deep softening of the skin, so that some parts of the body feel like silk to the touch.

Hair. Declining hair growth and pigmentation may result in thinning and/or graying hair in later years. While science has been helpful with a number of drugs that restore hair growth, and cosmetics have helped men and women cover up the gray, changes in hair growth and color accelerate as we grow older. I do have friends who have been successful with dignified silver, kicky gray and shocks of white, but that success seems to come from something inside themselves. They look great no matter what color hair they have.

Bones and muscles. More aches and pains, especially when we wake up in the morning – for me, that was the most persistent sign that I was approaching midlife. In addition, many of us find that we can break a bone at the drop of a hat when we had always considered ourselves pretty hardy otherwise. It may be harder to keep those abdominal muscles firm, more difficult to maintain muscle definition. These changes may be inevitable, but they are not irreversible. That is, vitamins, diet, and exercise can help minimize the effects of aging, helping to maintain muscle and bone mass and keeping muscles and connective tissue flexible. A few of my best friends have hard bodies at 40 and 50, both male and female.

Cardiovascular. Huffing and puffing. More and faster. That's what I noticed as I reached my 40s. Even though I've always exercised regularly, I was finding it harder to do as much as well. So what do you do about declining breath capacity and accelerated heart rates? You keep exercising, that's what. Not harder or more often. But maybe more consistently.

The senses. Bifocals are the big joke in my crowd. Every time someone else shows up to dinner with a new pair of glasses, we all get a big chuckle. No more holding the menu at arm's length. No more lifting the eyeglasses up and down. Sense of hearing, smell, and taste can also diminish with age. Many of us baby boomers are suffering loss of hearing from those ear-smashing rock concerts we frequented. Naturally, I listen to Enya more than Pete Townsend today.

So what do we do with this array of physical, body changes? Whatever we do, the decisions we make about how to deal with midlife physical changes require us to reflect on what our bodies are to us, and how we want to treat them. Do we see these changes as friendly guideposts to old age, or as warning signs of trouble ahead? Do we accept the changes, or try to hide them? Asking probing questions about how we feel about our bodies, and being conscious of all our decisions regarding this important aspect of ourselves, are critical to full wisdom and peace. Here are some questions that will prompt conscious thought about your body.

1. **How has your body been a friend to you throughout your life?** In what ways has your body performed for you? Is it possible to acknowledge your body's achievements? Recovery from serous illness might be one achievement. Maintaining good health. Giving you pleasure. What other ways can you acknowledge your body as a friend?

2. **How has your body been less than a friend?** If there have been ways that your body has seemed to turn on you, it might be helpful to acknowledge that, as well.

3. **How do you view your relationship with your body today?** You will know the answer to this question by observing how you talk to your body and by how you treat it.

4. **How has your body changed since you were 8? 18? 28?** How do you really feel about these changes?

5. **What do you love most about your body?** This may change as we age. Perhaps we were slender when we were younger and we loved the fact that no matter what we ate we would never gain weight. Maybe that has changed. And maybe there are new things to love about your body.

6. **Are you always aware of your body?** Many of us live in our heads more than in our bodies. Discover what percentage of your waking hours you are actually aware of your hands, your feet, your spine, your jaw, and other parts of your body. You might also discover what times of the day you are most body-conscious and what times of the day you are oblivious. You might want to discover, too, what brings you a vibrant awareness of your body.

7. **How do you thank your body?** Doing nice things for your body is obviously a way to thank it. You might want to find out from family and friends what they do to take care of themselves. I have girlfriends who do the most interesting things to their faces with fruit and vegetable packs and mixtures. While that isn't my thing on a regular basis, I might consider doing something like that for my body's birthday!

8. **How do you think others perceive your body? Is that important to you?** We say it's not important what others think. And we sometimes say looks aren't important. Nevertheless, I have received some of my most important information from friends willing to give me feedback about how I look. For instance, if a lot of people are telling me I look tired and worn out,

what is that saying to me? Am I tired and worn out? Is what others see an accurate reflection of me?

9. **If your body were to say something to you now, what would it say?** Is it tired and does it want you to slow down? Does it need more care, is it happy with the way you have treated it? Give your body a voice.

10. **What part of your body do you love most? What part do you love least?** How can you integrate the part you love most with the part you love least?

One of the most comforting things I know of for dealing with the physical changes that occur in midlife is joking with my midlife girlfriends. We've laughed until tears have rolled down our cheeks about plastic surgery, baggy eyelids, gray roots, and blue jeans that are going into the Blue Jean Hall of Fame (how did we ever get into those things?!). Deep reflection and inner work are valuable tools for dealing with change. And a sense of humor is indispensable.

Legacy/generativity

"A signal realization of middle age is…I am what survives me," observed psychologist Erik Erikson, in his book *Identity: Youth, and Crisis.* Erikson introduced the concept of generativity into the field of adult development in 1950, with his landmark book *Childhood and Society.* According to Erikson, once people have a sense of who they are and have established long-term, intimate relationships, they are then psychologically ready to make commitments and contributions to society as a whole – to its betterment and continuation. Therefore, with middle age may come a more altruistic bent, drawing us out of the self-preoccupation of youth and into the larger picture.

In fact, psychologists point to generativity as a human need from both biological and cultural standpoints. Biologically, procreation is driven by the need to regenerate and maintain the species. Culturally, generativity undergirds certain institutions, initiates social change, and encourages citizen contributions. The Sierra Club leans heavily on generativity from both fronts. To keep our species alive, they ask us to contribute to the Sierra Club and other environmental efforts.

The pitch has strong appeal. Even if we don't agree with Sierra Club politics, awareness of the connection between certain environmental contributions and the maintenance of the human species is a strong connection indeed.

Add a little ego to the idea of generativity and you get the idea of legacy – that which we leave behind not only to our friends and loved ones, but to the world at large. Sometimes we leave money behind. But most of us like to think we will be remembered for more than our money. We would like to be remembered for the unique personal contributions we have made to our families, friends, and communities.

But legacy isn't just a matter of ego. Stephen Covey points out in *First Things First* that there is a human need – a spiritual need – to transcend self. "The key to the fire within is our spiritual need to leave a legacy," he writes.

At midlife, there are a number of ways to take care of generativity and legacy needs. We may establish family traditions that reflect our philosophy or what we want to impart to our loved ones, such as the tradition my mother started about ten years ago at Thanksgiving. In a small jar, she placed a number of traditional Christian prayers written on colored paper, rolled and tied, and each year she passes the jar to whomever she thinks should read the prayer that year. This will be part of Mom's legacy – it's one thing we'll probably always remember when we remember her. Though it isn't a big thing, it's a Mom thing. At midlife, we may also wish to express our need to regenerate and leave a legacy through our volunteer efforts, or by participation in a church, or in politics. If we have retired, we may have more time for generative activities that don't necessarily generate lots of income (like writing a book).

When I coach my midlife clients through transition of any kind, I ask them questions that have to do with legacy – how they want to be remembered and what they want to leave behind. Once you know those things, you can begin living your life in alignment with your deeper purpose and convictions.

1. **What is your purpose? How are you fulfilling it?** If you haven't yet articulated your purpose, think of it as your mission, your reason for being. Companies say that their mission guides them to success. What is your reason for being here on earth? Speculate based on what you love to do, what you did with abandon in your youth, what people tell you that you are good at. Then determine why you think you came here, or were sent.

2. **What gifts have you received from others throughout your life?** Think especially about those who have died. Friends, relatives, mentors, spiritual leaders, political figures, beloved pets. Articulating the gifts they have left behind will get you thinking about your own legacy.

3. **What gifts have you given others?** Don't be modest. What people have told you about your gifts is true and real and the beginning of your legacy.

4. **What legacies have been most important to you in your life?** Thinking about people you most admire and determining which have meant the most to you will help you recognize what you may want to leave behind yourself.

5. **What three adjectives would describe how you want to be remembered?** Consider that you are in a group of people who don't know you are there, and that this group is talking about you. Now imagine adjectives that would be meaningful for you today.

6. **What three important things would you like mentioned in your eulogy?** You might even want to write your own eulogy or obituary in a way that would describe what you would consider to be a meaningful life for you. What would your friends or relatives say about you at your own funeral?

7. **How will your presence on earth make a difference in the lives of your family and friends, after you are gone?**

8. **What things can you do now to establish your legacy?** Think about traditions, messages and philosophies, values, and things you might want to give away.

9. **How are you contributing to the earth's supporting ecosystem?** If we are not paying attention to the responsibilities that are right in front of us, like recycling and conserving, our legacies are largely ego-based. To maintain the generations to come, there are some very simple, quiet things we can do to assure that our species will survive. Determine what those things are and set a quiet example for your family and neighbors. If you want to set a noisier example, join an environmental activist group, and get on a soapbox somewhere.

10. **What is left to accomplish, before you go?** Think about what needs to be done in the world, in your community, in your church or your political party, in your family, in your own life. Do you need to make a midlife *to-do* list now? Is stagnation even an option at this point in your life?

If you can remember that your legacy is your life, you will live with a more conscious connection to your family and friends; to your community, both local and global; and to yourself. Your soul journey will give you an opportunity to discover ways to embrace your immortality through the legacy of your life and the way you live it.

Spirituality

In her book *A Life Complete,* Sallirae Henderson suggests that an internal guide is indispensable to the uncertain middle years. "The internal guide must be in place and we must be skilled at using it before we arrive at the last years of our lives, when our losses will be many," she writes.

I think of the internal guide as my spirit – the intuitive, non-material part of myself with whom I consult from time to time, and who sustains me through difficult events. Without this guiding spirit, says Henderson, we may get lost. Drawing an analogy between the internal guide and a ship's navigational tools on a stormy sea, she tells us that this guide needs to be in place and fully functioning now, as we enter the second half of life. "Trying to find and learn how to use a compass is impossible when the vessel is overwhelmed by threatening seas," she says. "No craft would venture to enter unpredictable waters without having this expertise already in place."

Discovering or cultivating a relationship with our spiritual selves requires an inventory of our ideas concerning spirituality. Some of us have a hard time believing that spirit exists, because it's something we can't see. Even when there is heavy proof in the way of synchronicity and intuitive knowing, many shy away from ideas about spirituality, sometimes because it is not easy to understand and is therefore somewhat frightening, and sometimes because spirituality was presented in a bad light through past experiences, such as in the religion of family upbringing. Reconciling what we grew up with and what we know today is critical to developing internal, spiritual guidance.

So where do our ideas about spirituality come from? Church? Family? Personal experiences? Influential persons? My own ideas stem largely from my voracious curiosity about theological matters. I was raised in a Protestant church and had good experiences there. But I have read widely outside the church on religious traditions and philosophies, and as a result, my ideas have changed over the years. Fortunately, I've kept up with the changes and have stayed in touch with my internal guide. I have a church circuit of about five different churches, which keeps me on my toes. And I belong to a spirit-centered circle of friends and colleagues who honor and encourage a spiritual path. This is how I maintain my relationship with my spiritual self, or my internal guide. Finding a church, talking to friends, and taking time out to reflect are all critical to keeping my spiritual fires stoked.

1. **What is spirit?** Today, my own idea about spirit is that it is a unified field of consciousness with points within that represent individual spirit. The whole of the field represents God, for me, and I personify God when I want to communicate with him. Yes, for whatever reason, God is a male for me when it is time for me to talk to God. But I'm not saying God *is* male. I honor all the different perceptions of spirit. Defining in concrete terms your ideas about spirit may help you solidify the relationship with your internal guide.

2. **What adjectives would you use to describe your spirit?** Think color. Think texture. Think size and fragrance. Think outside the box.

3. **Where is your spirit?** Sometimes locating where your spirit lives helps you know it better. Mine lives somewhere in the middle of my physical body, near my heart. I heard someone share once that his spirit hung out in different parts of his house, like his backyard, waiting for him to connect.

4. **How long have you known your spirit?** Most relationships have histories, and knowing the history can shed light on the relationship. Determining when you first became conscious or communicative with your spirit can help you understand your current relationship.

5. **What other spirits are close to you? What adjectives would you use to describe each of them?** Again, think color, texture, size, and outside the box.

6. **What is more important – body, mind, spirit, or heart? Why?** Much has been written of late about the connection between body, mind, spirit, and heart. Even traditional medicine has embraced this connecting concept. But there may be one or more parts of you that have had a more important role in shaping your ideas and your place in the universe than other aspects. If so, discover what they are.

7. **How do you nurture your spirit today?** Just as we thank our bodies from time to time, we might want to consciously thank our spirits. After all, they have the potential of lightening our load, enlightening our mind, and setting us free. Perhaps they have done all three for you from time to time in your life. How do you say thank you?

8. **What does your spirit need?** Try asking it.

9. **Has your spirit changed since you were 8? 18? 28? If so, how?**

10. **Where did your spirit come from?** Pondering this question could lead you into deep theological philosophizing, which can be fun for some of us. Where did matter come from, for that matter? Just remember that it's just as important – perhaps more important – to live in and love the question as it is to find the answer.

Taking off for a sacred place with a heart receptive to discovering spirit can be a powerful, transforming experience. Pilgrims, be ready!

Finances

Reality usually catches up with us at midlife, on a number of fronts. Biological changes can make it difficult to deny the reality that we are moving into the second half of life. And if we haven't prepared financially for the shift, we may find ourselves shocked out of denial on the financial front, as well. Studies show that most baby boomers have neglected to save enough for a comfortable retirement and that for many of us, retirement will come in the form of inheritances from our parents – who, by the way, are living longer and requiring more financial assistance and time than anyone had ever anticipated. Many of us are facing uncertainty about our financial futures and are unsure what to do about it. Panic sets in. Is it too late to do anything to keep us from being bag ladies and men?

Through my private coaching practice and through my consulting with Drake, Beam, Morin, Inc., I have many career transition clients who are asked to take early retirement. Even major corporations who have employed people for up to 30 years sometimes ask them to leave without full benefit of the retirement fund they expected to receive. If they take less retirement income, early, they are at least assured of receiving some payment. If they fail to do so and are later laid off as a result of business decisions, they could be out in the cold entirely. Last year, I worked with a group of clients who had worked for one company for up to 35 years and who were told that in spite of layoffs, they would have a job…if they were willing to move to the East Coast. For people who have lived their whole lives in San Diego, with established families and communities, moving to the other side of the country at midlife was a frightening prospect. Some of my clients felt they had to brave this change in order to get to retirement safely. It is in times like these that money seems to be the cause of all our woes.

Even if we have prepared financially for the move into the second half of life, we face uncertainties in the form of potentially reduced social security, rising healthcare costs, unanticipated parental obligations, a restrictive job market, and spiraling inflation. These uncertainties can bring fear and discomfort if we aren't willing to look at our finances as friend rather than foe. In fact, even those of us who have a plentiful supply of money at hand may have a feeling of shortage, because of the fear money generates. If we want to live fear-free during our second half, we need to deal with our ideas about money.

In fact, I like Suze Orman's philosophy. She says in *The 9 Steps to Financial Freedom,* "The road to financial freedom begins not in a bank or even in a financial planner's office like mine, but in your head." Her book's subtitle is "Practical and Spiritual Steps So You Can Stop Worrying." Her spiritual approach to finances suggests that there's more to money than saving and spending it. Money represents something much larger in our lives and some of us have never dealt with what that "something" is. Now might be a good time.

In addition, then, to making sure you have a good financial planner and a good bank, you've got to get a good head full of thoughts about money, if you want to experience comfort during your middle years. Let's face it; we know that for some people, there is never enough money. So how *much* you have is not the answer.

1. **What has money given you in your lifetime thus far?** You might also ask the flip side of this question: what has it not given you. While money is a provider of many things, it is not the provider of everything. It's good to get it in perspective.

2. **How is money your best friend?** The answer to this question is similar to the first answer. Thinking about what money has provided, and what it has taught you, will help you see your finances in a positive light.

3. **Has money ever betrayed you? When?** Thinking about the past is a good way to explore your current relationship with money. Think about times when you thought you had money pegged and didn't really get it. How has money been more of a problem in your life and why?

4. **What adjectives would you use to describe your relationship with money when you were 8? 18? 28? Today?**

5. **What adjectives best describe the state of your finances today?** Think about adjectives that wouldn't ordinarily be used to describe finances. Soft and cuddly. Sharp and cutting. Baffling. Surprising. Come up with 10 or 12, if you can.

6. **How would you change your financial situation?** Besides "have more money," what other financial issues do you want to resolve? Organization of finances? Generativity?

7. **If you didn't need the money and possessions you have today, what would you do with them?** Think of all the things you could do with them. Think in terms of legacy and generativity.

8. **When are you most aware of the flow and energy that money represents? How can you bring that awareness to your daily events?** Are you conscious

about money? Are your bills neatly organized in your wallet, your checkbook up to date? Are you aware on a daily basis of how much money is in your bank account? Answers to these questions will help you understand how and why your money acts the way it does.

9. **What do you need to do to put your financial matters in order?** This might be a time to think about a step-by-step process for setting your mind at ease when it comes to finances.

10. **How will finances be part of your legacy?** Whether you have a lot of money, or only a little, think about the role it will play in your leaving. Think about your will, your material treasures, and your level of generosity versus your level of fear. How will people remember you when it comes to money?

Self-reflection can be considered an investment in your peace of mind. The return may be surprising, because it can manifest in many ways – including financial abundance!

Relationships

At midlife, friends and family are as important as the internal guide Sallirae Henderson describes in her book *A Life Complete.* These primary relationships will help point us to True North, and they will sustain us through the losses typical in the second half of life. If we haven't learned how to cultivate deep and meaningful relationships by now, we need to begin right away.

Relationships have provided me with the deepest lessons of life, lessons I've had to dig for. Over the years I have had to learn to drop judgment, take my own inventory, listen actively, make love my bottom line, be empathetic, compassionate, and sympathetic. I've also had to learn to set boundaries, say no, and walk away. Whew.

As a result, today my life is less filled with the high drama that once caused me so much stress, and I am at peace with every relationship in my life. I own a business with my sister, who is my one of my dearest friends. My daughter and I are dearest friends, too, and I don't mind saying she is just about my favorite person on earth. My mom and I are dear friends, though I wouldn't say we are exactly close nor have we ever been. But we've worked through the turmoil that once defined our relationship. I have other dear male and female friends, and I think I'm even friends with myself. I will say that I'm not married and that may be because I realize it's the most difficult of relationships and I am possibly not up for the challenge. I'm not perfect in the area of relationships, but I'm pleased with my progress.

If you think it was easy to get here, though, think again. Seven years ago I wasn't speaking to my mom, and my daughter wasn't speaking to me. My sister and I weren't in business together and though we loved each other, we had trouble really communicating. I had an unfulfilling romantic relationship and I didn't get along very well with my boss. With a great deal of therapy, mentoring, spiritual questing, journaling, making amends, and learning, I've come to the point where my primary relationships are the most important things in life to me, plain and simple. They require time and effort, but the payoff is tremendous. I've thought about them, written about them, cried about them, and watched them grow. And now I expect that my relationships will truly sustain me throughout the second half of my life. Furthermore, while I sometimes get thrown for a loop by things that are said between me and my friends, I intuitively know what to do. Love is my bottom line and I let it guide me.

Exploring our primary relationships (family, friends, some co-workers, and various kinds of partners) as well as our secondary relationships (co-workers, doctors, lawyers, acquaintances), yields a personal perspective on life that is rich and that tells us a lot about ourselves. I suggest probing for answers to the following questions.

1. **Which are your primary relationships? Describe each one.** Try describing each one in detail. How long have you had each of these relationships? What is the history behind them? How important is each, on a scale of 1–10, with 1 being quite unimportant and 10 being critical? What does each relationship give you? What does it allow you to give? What have your learned from each?

2. **How have your relationships changed since you were 8? 18? 28? Today?**

3. **Where do primary relationships fit among your priorities?** You can tell how important these relationships are by the amount of time you spend on improving them, and how much time you spend with the other person or people in the relationship. If you had the opportunity to make a big chunk of change, or the opportunity to spend quality time with one of your primary relationships, under what circumstances would you choose either one?

4. **Do relationships always take place between and among people? What other things are you in relationship with?** Since I like to think of the spirit world as the sum total of all interconnected things, I sometimes think of my relationship with the hummingbirds that hover around my front deck, and my relationship with the trees outside my front window, as some of my primary relationships. I also have a relationship with my home; it shelters me and in turn I have to maintain it. There is a mutual responsibility there. Think about all the things you are connected to in your life, living or not, and how you are in relationship with them.

5. **How is your relationship with the universe?** You'll be able to answer this question by looking at your altruistic efforts, and by checking out how your treat the environment. You'll also be able to tell if you have a good relationship by what the universe has offered you. Safety? Joy? Dream fulfillment? Enlightenment?

6. **How is your relationship with yourself?** Some say this is the most important relationship, and I don't doubt it. When you think about your relationship with yourself, consider how you treat yourself, speak to yourself, how much time you spend with yourself, what your expectations are, and what you can do to improve the relationship.

7. **What is the connection between your relationship with the universe and your relationship with yourself?** It might be interesting to look at your relationship with yourself to see if it is reflected in any way with your relationship with the universe. In other words, if you aren't getting along particularly well with yourself, you may find that the universe feels like a more hostile place.

8. **How can you improve some of your work relationships?** Be specific. Which ones could use improvement, and how?

9. **How can you improve some of your family relationships?** Even if a relationship feels good to you, how can you make it even more fulfilling for everyone?

10. **What other kinds of relationships do you want to add to your life?** There's no need to stop bringing new relationships into your life. People remarry at midlife. We even have kids at this stage of our lives. We get new pets. We buy new homes. We don't want to add relationships indiscriminately, but there's nothing wrong with a rich and diverse array of new primary relationships at midlife and beyond.

Believe me, for the past year or so, I have been thinking long and hard about the lack of romantic relationships in my own life. As I consider ways to close the gap here, I realize there's more to my awareness than simply wanting someone to share life with, though that is certainly a lofty desire and something I want today. But I am also very clear that my resistance and unwillingness to pursue and maintain these kinds of relationships hold profound lessons for me. So I still have lessons to learn and I suspect the next ones will come as a result of my willingness to enter into romantic intimacy.

This discovery comes as a delight to me. That I am called upon to continue facing inner challenges means that I have more untapped potential, that I can become a fuller and wiser woman, even at midlife.

Priorities

Stephen Covey says in *First Things First* that "It's easy to say 'no!' when there's a deeper 'yes!' burning inside." For me, this is the Number One time management principle. Knowing what fuels my soul and stoking that fire continually gives me all the guidelines I need for making choices about how to spend my time.

Midlife may be a perfect time to re-evaluate and re-articulate your priorities, because priorities change. At one time, my career was the top priority. Sadly, I think it may have even taken precedence over raising my daughter, at times.

Today, my soul is top priority – keeping everything in order and abiding by the guiding principles I have identified for myself. Second is family and friends; third is community; and today, career is fourth. My attention and time are divided accordingly. For many of us, adventure and fun are priorities in youth, and not so much in middle age. I have a number of friends, however, for whom adventure and fun are a *new* priority. And it's been important for them to discover that.

To articulate priorities, I suggest evaluating your principles, vision, values, and mission.

Principles are one's guiding ethics. Many religions articulate a set of principles and you may even want to start there. Examine the Koran, the Ten Commandments, the Golden Rule, the Dhamma-pada, or the sayings of Confucius. Which ones ring true for you? Which ones are guiding your life? Which need to be given more consideration in your life today? Making a list of these principles and writing about them will help solidify them for you and make them operative in your life.

Vision is the life-dream residing deep within you. It is the way you see your life unfolding in the future. It's all the things you want from your life, and all the things you want to give life. I suggest being very specific about your vision for your life. Write about it as if you were writing a story about your life – where you are in this vision, who else is there, the feeling in the air, the colors and sounds surrounding you. What are you doing in your vision? This is an exhilarating, empowering place to be, because it is not something you are conjuring, it's not a fiction you are imagining. What Kahlil Gibran said about children is also true about our dreams – they come *through* us, but are not from us.

Drawn from your guiding principles, *values* are inner qualities that have great, intrinsic worth to you. You may value honesty, for instance, above all else, or beauty, or discipline. One good way to determine your values is to make a list of as many things as you can think of that you value. List up to 25 or 30 or more things, and then narrow that list to your Top Ten Values, those qualities that must be present in order for you to feel comfortable with another person and with yourself.

Mission is your raison d'être. It's also called *purpose.* You can determine your life mission by examining your past. What have you been drawn to do in the past? What has given you pleasure? A colleague of mine always points me to age ten and says, "What was your favorite thing to do back then?" Whatever you've received most pleasure from is closely connected to your mission. You see, the good news is that we are here to be happy. It's up to us to know what makes us happy.

Once you've given some thought to principles, vision, values, and mission, your priorities will become clear. Articulating them will be relatively easy. Here are some questions to help you.

1. **Have you identified your priorities? If yes, what are your top three? If not, why not?** Knowing what your *top three* priorities are, if you have identified your priorities, may be difficult. But try. Knowing why you *haven't* identified and articulated your life's priorities may be very telling. An exercise in and of itself.

2. **What were your top three priorities when you were 8? 18? 28? How have they changed?**

3. **How do you know what your priorities are?** When you are confronted with a number of choices, how do you know which ones to pick? What are your guides?

4. **How often do you evaluate your priorities? Is this often enough?** I suggest to the people I coach that they evaluate their priorities when they feel stressed out, when they are making a big decision, and regularly, whether they need to or not!

5. **How are your priorities reflected in the way you live your life?** If you look at your life today, your current priorities will be clear. How much time you spend on things is a good indication of what you find worthy.

6. **Do any of your priorities conflict? If so, how? And how does the conflict affect your peace of mind?** For almost all of us, priorities will conflict at one time or another. For instance, meditation is a priority for me because my soul work comes first, above all else. It's important for me to clear my mind and to speak to my heart in order for my soul to feel fed and in order. However, from time to time my daughter or sister or a dear friend will call during my meditation

time, with a problem or a need, or my cat will jump on my lap for attention. Telling my daughter that I'm busy meditating and getting my soul in order seems inappropriate. Locking my cat in the next room is out of the question. I just integrate my priorities and realize that everything feeds my soul. One person has suggested to me that I get up earlier to meditate. Most people don't call before 7:00 a.m., regardless of their need to talk. However, another priority is the seven to eight hours of sleep I need each night. I compromise that occasionally, but to stay healthy and well balanced, I need that sleep as much as I need to meditate. While these kinds of conflicts can present challenges to the mind and to the clock, I've learned just to go with the flow most of the time. If meditation time is getting cut off too often, I make adjustments. Life happens and can't always be prioritized and managed.

7. **Do others understand your priorities?** Relationships can be strained if our colleagues and loved ones don't understand why something is important to us. You might have to explain. Determine which relationships could use a good priority discussion.

8. **How do your priorities affect your relationships?** Sometimes this is a question of time management. What's more important? Your wife or your job? Your career or your boyfriend? If relationships are tense, it might be that you are too focused on priorities and not focused enough on people.

9. **How do your priorities affect your work?** Again, this can be a matter of time management. If your priorities include plenty of leisure time and your boss is getting tired of your requests for time off, your priorities are affecting your work.

10. **How do your priorities define who you are?** Think about your priorities and whether they aptly describe who you are as a person.

My own mission statement is "*to encourage and facilitate inner work*," and from there flow my priorities. My daughter's mission statement is "*to reach out and touch those less fortunate than I.*" My landscaping client Bert says he is here "*to tend God's green earth.*" What is your mission statement?

Loose ends

Whenever I go in for a tune-up with my psychotherapist, I inevitably find issues from the past that I need to tend to. If I'm not getting along with my boyfriend, it has something to do with things I never said but should have said to an old boyfriend, or to my father. If I spend too much money too often, it's because I didn't get to buy the kind of prom dress I thought I wanted, and had to wear one my mom made for me (though my mom made beautiful gowns on her Singer sewing machine). To take care of these "hanging issues," as my therapist describes them, I have to tie them up somehow. I write a letter to the old boyfriend; I buy a dress I really want and tell myself it's my "prom dress."

In addition, there are just things I need to take care of that I have been putting off, perhaps for years! From fixing the garage door to putting photos in the family album, these unfinished projects can have a stalling effect on my psyche. With my conscious or unconscious cluttered and bogged down with loose ends, it's hard for me to move forward until I tie them up, because I keep tripping over them, and I feel somehow incomplete.

When I started coaching, one of my first clients had a difficult time completing her assignments. Though these were assignments she had created and signed up for on her own, whenever we got on the phone for our coaching session, she had several reasons for not completing them, and almost all of her reasons had to do with housecleaning. She had to clean out the refrigerator, dust the wall-to-wall shutters throughout her house, clean all the mirrored walls and doors, polish the silverware. All of these tasks got in the way of the steps she was taking to change careers.

I had her make a list of all the housecleaning projects she needed to take care of, and built them into her weekly assignments. So instead of repotting all the dying plants, repainting the deck, cleaning out the fireplace, and dusting under the refrigerator all in one week, she agreed to take one or two of these tasks and complete them, along with her other assignments.

Early in my coaching career, I began asking my clients to make a list of unfinished projects and incomplete relationships as part of our needs assessment, because I have learned that these loose ends can stand in the way of progress toward larger, more important goals. Sometimes the list of loose ends is monumental. Then I ask my clients to prioritize the discomfort level they have with each item on the list. The ones that are really bugging them are the ones we include in our coaching goals over a three-month period.

In order to move forward at midlife, we need to clean out our project closet and determine what loose ends need to be tied up. We can enter the second half of life uncluttered and clean with just a little tidying up. Here are some of the questions I ask my clients to answer as part of our needs assessment.

1. **What relationships still need to be mended?** There are a number of relationships throughout life that may get left dangling. We got mad and walked out of them; we didn't say the things we really needed to say; we said the wrong things and now that we know better, there are the things we need to say now. Making a list of broken relationships and then determining how to mend them can be healing and can clear the way toward progress in other areas of life.

2. **What relationships do you need to re-establish?** If we have let go of important relationships because we were too busy, or because of a misunderstanding, we may feel the need to bring that relationship back into our lives. It may feel like a missing link, otherwise.

3. **What financial matters still need to be addressed?** At midlife, we need to consider our own self-supporting efforts, including long-term health insurance, extended care insurance, and vacation funds. We also need to make sure we have written a will. There may be other financial matters we've been putting off – finding out what's in our social security fund, developing an investment strategy for the second half of life. Now's the time.

4. **What family matters are still hanging?** Even if we have moved on from family misunderstandings, if they are covered over but not resolved they may constitute a loose end. If the family hasn't developed a plan for taking care of mom in her old age, or taking care of you in *your* old age, that may need to be addressed, as well. How to share responsibility for aging parents, how to deal with legal matters, how to deal with burials and funerals, how to mend conflicts and nagging interpersonal tensions – all these should be considered as you tie up loose ends.

5. **Have you lost anything that you stopped looking for? What is it? Where might it be?** About a year ago, my girlfriend Sara gave up looking for the opal brooch her grandmother had willed to her. She assumed it had fallen out of her jewelry box in a cross-country move she had made. But the loss was deep. Sara had loved her grandmother, who had told her since childhood that the brooch would someday be hers. From time to time, the guilt of losing the heirloom crept up on Sara. I asked her to sit down and think again about where it might be, so that she could be absolutely certain that there was no place else to look. She decided to give it one last try, to go through about a dozen boxes in her garage – boxes where the brooch might have lodged during packing. And there it was, at the bottom of one box crammed with old sketchbooks and art tools, of all things. Sara tells me she's sure the brooch was speaking to her through her guilt, nagging her to come find it. She has a sense of freedom now that her brooch is found. Even if she hadn't found it, knowing that she had done all she could to look for it, and then perhaps replacing it with something meaningful, would have helped her tie up that particular loose end.

6. **What memories do you need to document?** I'm terrible at putting my photos in albums. I have a big white wicker chest, and I just throw them in there (in envelopes), thinking. . . someday! Fifteen years worth of photos will take me years to organize. Luckily, I don't care. It doesn't bother me. It's an extremely low priority. But for some people, this sort of project looms over them and takes over a nice big corner of their psyche. Take time to determine what memories you need to organize or release to notebook or art project.

7. **What needs to be fixed at your home?** This is a delightful list. You've been trying to forget about these things! Bring them to the light of day and develop a plan for getting them done.

8. **What health issues have you been ignoring?** You've been meaning to ask the doctor about natural hormones. You have a nagging ache in your lower back. You seem to be tired all the time. Your doctor told you to get that mole removed three years ago. Taking care of your health takes time. As busy midlifers, we sometimes put these things aside hoping they will go away. They don't. They just hang around and bug our unconscious mind.

9. **What letters do you need to write?** Did you ever answer the letter Aunt Mabel wrote you three years ago? Do you need to complain to the customer service department in writing about the poor performance of your garbage disposal? Do you need to write the credit bureaus to clear up a mistake on your report? Go ahead. Make a list of the letters you need to write and determine when you're going to get them done.

10. **What other loose ends do you need to acknowledge?**

While it's important to make an inventory of your loose ends, it's just as important to pull together a plan for tying them up. I ask my clients to prioritize the extent of their discomfort with items on the Loose Ends list and I ask them to determine which ones need to be tied up in the next three months, along with a plan for tying them up. It's an organized, practical approach to internal housecleaning.

Forgiveness

In *Further Along the Road Less Traveled,* popular psychologist M. Scott Peck says, "The process of forgiveness – indeed, the chief reason for forgiveness – is selfish." What he proceeds to tell us is that we forgive others not for *their* sake, but for our own, because, "if we hold on to our anger, we stop growing and our souls begin to shrivel."

When someone does us harm, the normal reaction is a certain amount of anger. That reaction is a product of our "fight or flight" instinct, a primitive drive to protect ourselves and our territory. If someone impinges on us, we are either scared, or – more often – we are mad.

Living with anger blocks what Bill W. called "The Sunlight of the Spirit" in the book *Alcoholics Anonymous.* That's why the Twelve Step Programs are so adamant about eradicating "resentments." They are the "number one offender," according to the A.A. literature. If alcoholics don't get rid of resentments, they are sure to drink again, according to the program.

My own spiritual mentor points out to me that getting mad isn't the problem. It's staying mad that's the problem. She says that if we hang on to our anger well past its usefulness, it becomes a resentment. And it blocks the Sunlight of the

Spirit. Anger is useful when it prompts us to go to someone and let them know what's on our mind. It's useful when we've really been done harm and need to have it rectified. Beyond that, it's useless. And it shrivels the soul.

My own therapist once told me I would never be able to move forward until I forgave my mother. Forgive my mom? She was sick! She was mentally ill and she did the best she could! I'd moved on, and it wasn't about forgiveness. But with a lot of gentle prodding, my therapist helped me realize that not only had my mother been mentally ill – she didn't need forgiveness for that – she had been cruel and unavailable. For that she needed forgiveness. It was difficult going back and recalling how cruel she had been, and how unavailable. But it was true. And I realized that I needed to give her real forgiveness, not what Dr. Peck calls the "cheap forgiveness" of "she did the best she could." It was good for me to realize she did the best she could, but that isn't forgiveness.

Forgiving is not forgetting. In fact, humans often "forget" or repress incidents that are particularly painful, and they may repress without even knowing it. Forgiving is a conscious act that requires not only awareness of the act that requires forgiveness, but also awareness of our own human frailties. As Dr. Peck points out, when Jesus said, "Judge not that ye be not judged," he wasn't saying, "Don't ever judge anyone." He was just letting us know that every time we judge someone, we open ourselves to judgment as well. In fact, Jesus went on to let us know we need to look at our own failings first so that we can see the "mote" in our brother's eye more clearly. So forgiveness is an act of humility and kindness, and it requires tenderness in its execution.

If you have reached midlife and do not have forgiveness, you are endangering your soul. Don't wait another minute. Now is the time to explore the power of forgiveness in your life.

1. **What does it mean to forgive?** Try writing a definition. Look up the word in the dictionary. Check it out in a thesaurus and determine what the opposite of forgiveness is.
2. **Who have you forgiven in your life?** There may be many people you've had to forgive in your life. You may have made a conscious effort to do this, or you may have forgiven fully without ever going through a conscious forgiveness

process. Make yourself aware of all the people who have hurt you at one time or another and determine if they have been forgiven.

3. **Who do you need to forgive now?** If you shine a light inside that heart of yours, you may find some scratchy, uncomfortable feelings that could be translated into resentment. If so, explore whether forgiveness is an appropriate response.

4. **What is difficult about forgiving?** Forgiving always seems to be easier said than done. Asking yourself why you can or can't forgive someone is helpful.

5. **Must you forgive?** Some religious traditions suggest that forgiveness is an imperative, that if we are to be forgiven we must forgive. I once had a physician tell me that a particular chronic illness might be caused by unforgiveness. While I thought this was absurd at the time, I realize today that my body and soul are inextricably interconnected, and that the doctor's advice makes sense. Explore your own personal and religious convictions about the concept of forgiveness. Is it a universal law?

6. **What will happen if you don't forgive?** Consider what you gain from holding on to "unforgiveness." Consider what you gain from letting go of your resentment and opening your heart to forgiveness.

7. **How do you forgive?** Pretend you're writing an article on forgiveness titled "Three Steps to Forgiveness." Write about these steps and ask yourself if there is an opportunity for you to apply these steps to any relationship in your life.

8. **How does it feel to forgive?** Think of the people you have forgiven in your life. Write down adjectives describing how it feels when forgiveness is accomplished.

9. **Who has forgiven you? How do you know?** We need to be forgiven as much as we need to forgive. While you can never force someone to forgive you, you can at least make an effort to express sincere regret for hurts you have

caused. Go back as far as you can and figure out who you've hurt, how you've made up for it, and whether you've been forgiven. If you think you have been forgiven, how can you be sure? If you haven't, is there something you need to do?

10. **Do you need to forgive yourself? For what?** My mentors always tell me I'm harder on myself than anyone else they know. So every night when I do my evening inventory – "Where have I been dishonest or unkind, and who do I need to say 'sorry' to?" – I include my actions toward myself in the question.

There's nothing like a relationship that has experienced the clean sweep of forgiveness. Mom and I may not be best friends today, but we would both do anything we could to help each other, with no reservations, with generosity and genuine love. My heart's much lighter, my tongue so much kinder, in the presence of my forgiven mom.

Worldview

We assume that the world just is. It exists for me and for everyone else in just the same way.

This may not be true at all. In fact, many spiritual masters tell us that the world we live in is the world as we see it. We have all sorts of assumptions about the world that others don't have, and *my* assumptions about the world may be in direct conflict with what *you* assume about the world. Examining our worldview helps us understand ourselves and others.

By the time we reach midlife, we have accumulated a boatload of assumptions about the world. Examining those assumptions and being aware of how we view the world in ways that may be different from the way others view the world, results in wisdom. Owning our view of the world and allowing others to own theirs not only results in tolerance and deeper understanding, but in a release from fear, because we can change our assumptions – we can change the way we view the world. And that means that we are not victims of the world; we are not powerless over our lives. We can change the world we live in by seeing it differently.

Shapers of worldview include religion, societal and cultural beliefs, family, influential people in our lives, influential philosophers or writers, profound experiences, pivotal insights, inspirational guides, and inner guides. Knowing how each of these shaping elements has influenced our worldview helps us understand the world itself.

While an examination of worldview is a profoundly philosophical experience that requires deep thought and self-examination, the evaluation can bring forth the wisdom that is uniquely yours.

1. **Are we born with evil tendencies? Or do we learn them?** Think of the babies you have known. Are they sweet and perfect? Or are they self-centered and demanding? Do they know how to be of service? What capacities for love are we born with and what capacities do we have to cultivate over our lifetimes?

2. **How did the earth get here? How did you get here?** A very fundamental question indeed. You will not have the definitive answer by the time your pilgrimage is over, but you may know what you believe.

3. **Is there a Higher Power always present and available to you?** Knowing what you believe about God is an important aspect of wisdom and something you may want or need to articulate for future generations at some time. Based on your experiences, you should be able to come up with some ideas about how to answer this question for yourself.

4. **Are most people generally cheering for your success, or are they mostly cheering for your demise? Or are they ambivalent?** I had a friend who told me that at one time, she looked at the world as a hostile place. Once she started believing that everyone was pulling for her instead of against her, life changed. She went around telling herself that everyone she met wanted her to be successful and happy. As a result, she became a wildly successful author and public speaker with a multitude of friends, who knew her as a sunny, positive force in their lives.

5. **Must we compete to survive? Or must we collaborate?** This is the same as asking whether there is enough in the world for everyone, or whether

everything is scarce. If your worldview is one in which you are in competition for the limited resources that exist in the world – from emotional resources to food and shelter – you will behave differently than if your world has more than enough and all you have to do is share what you have and there will be more.

6. **What role does humanity play in relation to nature?** The question about whether humanity is here to fix nature, to improve upon nature, to live in harmony with nature, to take care of it, or simply to admire it, is another age-old question and even those who consider themselves ardent environmentalists find it hard to agree. So have fun exploring this one. Are you here to take care of the trees? Or are they here to take care of you?

7. **Why are we here?** Examining your larger purpose as a member of the human species is another question that's been batted around for ages.

8. **Does good always triumph over evil? Or is it the other way around?** Questions about good and evil can define our worldview quite a bit. Which is the stronger force in your life? Which wins out most often?

9. **Where did your beliefs about the world come from?** Naming these shapers of worldview will help you better understand why you see things the way you do. Your worldview is not of you; it flows *through* you but comes from hundreds of sources. What makes it uniquely yours is your synthesis of all the things that have come your way, filtered through your own personal experiences. Though your worldview has been shaped by outside forces, it is, indeed, your very own.

10. **How have your beliefs about the world changed since you were 8? 18? 28?**

Having discovered your worldview through searching and probing, you may think your work is done. Not so. Your worldview is not static but continually evolving. When I was a child, I lived in a world that included a tooth fairy, an Easter bunny, and an all-knowing Santa Claus, along with various other mystical creatures. As each of these fantasies faded, my worldview became less magical and more grounded in material realities. However, over the past several years, mystery and enchantment have slowly re-entered my life with spiritual realities. As we approach the second half of life, our worldview may once again reflect our younger and sometimes more intuitive perceptions. I look forward to the continual evolution of my own worldview.

3

Personal Pilgrimage

How do we make the time to explore the issues identified in the previous chapter? Some people make long pilgrimages to explore their hearts and souls. One of my favorite pilgrim figures is Peace Pilgrim, who at the age of 44 decided to chuck the conventionalities of being a housewife and to walk for peace. This was a brave thing to do in the 1950s, when most women were firmly entrenched in the roles of wife and mother, and womanly quests were limited to finding the best supermarket bargains. Her real name was Mildred Norman. After hiking the entire 2050-mile length of the Appalachian Trail in 1952, she had a vision that instructed her to keep walking and to talk about nothing but peace – peace in the world and peace within. Peace was her one and only issue. Her speeches and writing portray her personal quest for the truth about peace, and her desire to share it. She crossed the United States six times in her lifetime.

In order to quest, Peace Pilgrim removed herself from her everyday surroundings, for life. She walked incredibly long distances and deprived herself in order to stay focused on her journey – she had one set of clothes and carried nothing but a comb, a folding toothbrush, a pen, and her peace leaflets to pass out along the way.

As postmodern midlifers, we can take a lesson from Peace Pilgrim, but we don't have to go quite so far. Taking ourselves away from the personal communication equipment to which we sometimes feel chained, and traveling light for a few hours at a time, we can have momentous *aha* moments and peaceful time for inner exploration. I refer to these shorter versions of pilgrimage as the *personal pilgrimage.*

There are many definitions of pilgrimage and many ways to think about it. One of Merriam Webster's definitions calls pilgrimage "the course of life on earth." But generally speaking, a pilgrimage is considered a journey one makes to a sacred site or shrine, in order to find enlightenment, healing, or wholeness. While the traditional pilgrimage may call us to an exotic, faraway site, today's postmodern personal pilgrimage gives us the opportunity to seek without traveling far. A personal pilgrimage allows us to get in touch with the sacred that exists right outside our own back doors. We can incorporate traditional customs and rituals, along with the four phases of traditional pilgrimage, into a one-day soul journey that serves the same purpose as the longer, more planning-intense sojourns we have come to think of as pilgrimages.

Pilgrimage rituals

In this postmodern age, with its quick and superficial sequence of facts and events, I think it is more important than ever to slow the clock from time to time and experience the mysteries of life through spiritual ritual. Those of us who have forgotten how, or who feel we don't have the time, are missing a part of life that is born of the ancient soul. From pre-historic times, ritual has played a central role in the spiritual life of all cultures. When we cut ourselves off from ritual, we lose the continuity of the human experience and the opportunity to make everyday things sacred.

Two rituals have been built into the personal pilgrimage: the selection of a gift and a coin to leave at each pilgrimage site you visit. Both are traditional pilgrimage rituals. You can create other rituals or you can use those that have been created by others. Books that might help you include *Everyday Rituals and Ceremonies* by Lorna St. Aubyn, and Cathyann Fisher's *Sacred Ceremonies: Rituals for the Soul.* One of my favorite ritual books is *Mother Earth Spirituality* by Ed McGaa.

Music, incense, candles, sacred text, journaling, prayers, chants, dance, poetry – all provide building blocks for rituals that can nurture your ancient and postmodern soul. Here are some ideas.

FLOWERS

- Fill your house with multi-colored flowers the night before your personal pilgrimage, or for your homecoming. Think of them as symbols of the beautiful thoughts that will fill your heart and mind before, during, and after your journey. Speak words of love to your flowers as you prepare them for their vases and place them around your house.
- The night before your journey, spread flower petals in front of your altar, on a

Sacred Customs

The Personal Pilgrimage Templates contained in Part 2 of this book will provide you with some guidance and written exercises, but in postmodern fashion, they will also encourage you to pull out your own meditation techniques, your own favorite music and incense, your own ideas, so that you can customize your pilgrimage to meet your own unique needs. You may wish to select pilgrimage clothing, for example, so that when the family sees you donning your green flannel shirt or your baseball cap, they know you're on *personal pilgrimage.* You may wish to fast. Or not. Make an all-night vigil before your pilgrimage. Or not. You decide.

The Index of Inspirational Guides contained in Part 3 of this book provides a source of wisdom and inspiration for your journey. You might think of the guides listed in the index as the focal point of your pilgrimage, as traditional pilgrims might focus on St. Patrick during treks to the sacred mountain of Croagh Patrick in Ireland, or as many are drawn to Mother Meera for their pilgrimages to Thalheim, Germany. On the other hand, your guides may simply help you think about someone besides your boss or your clients while you are on *personal pilgrimage.* In any event, you may select a name from the index or choose one not included there. A form is provided in the index for outlining the biography of a guide not included in the index.

The index was prepared to address the multiculturalism of a postmodern age and includes individuals from many walks of life, representing different life perspectives, different philosophies, and different viewpoints. The persons included in the index are some who have inspired me during my own personal pilgrimages. It is not an exhaustive list and does not represent every world culture, religion, or race. It is a starting point, if you wish to use it. But by all means, if you feel an attraction to a personage not listed in the index, explore. The mini-biographies that compose the index are intentionally sparse and relatively free

nearby pillow, or in front of your doorway (or all three!). After your journey, place them in your journal.

- Find a single flower that calls out to you, place it in a bud vase beside your bed, and pay special attention to it as you retire the night before your journey and the night of your return.

DANCE

- Find colorful scarves and exotic music. Play the music and swirl the scarves as you glide around the room before you begin your night-before preparations.
- Before you begin your night-before preparations, find music conducive to the ambience you want to create, stand with your eyes closed, and sway to the rhythm, concentrating on the movement within.
- Try dancing without music for one to three minutes, as you prepare the night before.

SOUND

- Play happy, rambunctious music as loud as you dare when you return from your journey (you may need your earphones).
- Find finger cymbals (some alternative bookstores will have them) and use them before and after prayer.
- Find a special tape or CD that you always play the night before and for your homecoming.
- Sing or chant certain songs during the night before.

CANDLES

- Fill the room with lit candles the night before or after your journey. Turn out all the electrical lights and meditate by candlelight.

- Find one taper. Bless it as your pilgrimage candle and use it for the night of your preparation or your homecoming. Each time you light it, say a special prayer.
- After lighting a candle, stand in the doorway through which you will leave and return, holding the candle high and asking a Higher Power to bless your journey.

PRAYER AND MEDITATION

- Write a special pilgrimage prayer and use it to begin each phase of your journey: heeding the call, preparation, the journey, and the homecoming.
- Select words of wisdom from one of the Inspirational Guides in this book and write them with flourishes on a piece of elegant paper. Place the paper on a pillow, on your altar, or in a special place in the room where you will be preparing for your journey and contemplate the words throughout your pilgrimage.
- Find a different mantra for each pilgrimage and use it during various times of journaling and meditation.

OTHER

- Select special clothing or a certain hat that you always wear on your personal pilgrimages.
- Before your journey, stand in front of the doorway with a stick of incense or a sprig of sage. Wave the fragrance toward all four corners of the door, asking for blessings on your journey from all directions.
- Write a thank you letter upon your return to your Higher Power, to Mother Nature, to your Higher Self, to the Universe, or to whomever you would like to thank. Place it in an envelope with the name of the proposed recipient and mail it the next day.

of editorial comment, allowing you to make up your own mind about the guide's contributions, and to embellish what has been written here with your imagination, your prior knowledge, or your additional research. The idea is to focus on the contribution this person's life has made to the world you live in today, not on the differences between your point of view and theirs. Although the differences are important, even more so are the similarities.

The templates will also suggest that you select gifts to either leave at your pilgrimage site or somewhere en route. This custom parallels the gift custom of the traditional pilgrimage. For example, pilgrims leave food at Bali temples and at Tibetan monasteries. At the Vietnam Veterans Memorial in Washington D.C., pilgrims leave personal mementos, photographs, flags, and flowers. White ribbons adorn the holly bushes around the Chalice Well in Glastonbury, England. Gifts may commemorate the personage honored at a pilgrimage site, or they may serve as thank-you tokens for safe arrival and deep experiences.

Just be sure you are not leaving something behind that will detract in any way from the natural state in which you find your pilgrimage destination. If it does, consider leaving the gift at a local thrift store, school, nursing home, or social agency on the way home from your pilgrimage.

Another very important pilgrimage custom is the blessing. In ancient times, journeys to far-off places were considered so dangerous travelers might never return. Therefore, they simply did not leave on pilgrimage without a blessing. Pilgrims asked priests and other holy people to lay hands on their heads, anoint their feet, and utter elegant phrases that would send them safely on their way. While we may be physically safer in our voyaging, today's pilgrims still seek the good wishes of those they love, and prayers for spiritual sustenance and overall safekeeping.

A final custom I would like to suggest is one that could help connect postmodern pilgrims who have taken on the practice of personal pilgrimage. I suggest that you leave behind a coin of some type in an unobtrusive spot, yet where it could still be sighted by another pilgrim. In other words, if you arrive at your destination and find a coin somewhere near, it may be that this spot has been visited by another postmodern pilgrim. The coin signifies exchange. It signifies unity and interconnection. If you find more than two coins at the site, you might want to pick them up, recycle them in a meaningful way, and leave only yours behind.

The Four Phases of Pilgrimage

While the pilgrimage templates contained in Part 2 are each different, they each take you through the four phases of a traditional pilgrimage.

I. HEEDING THE CALL

In this phase of your personal pilgrimage, you hear your own cry for clarity, for space. In response, you do four simple things.

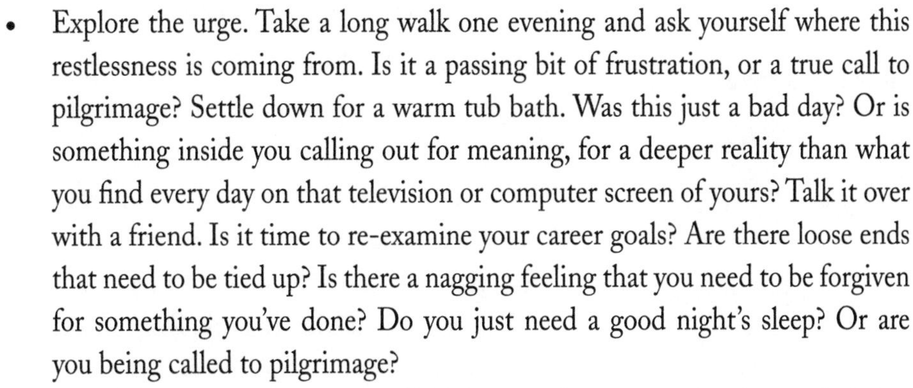

- Explore the urge. Take a long walk one evening and ask yourself where this restlessness is coming from. Is it a passing bit of frustration, or a true call to pilgrimage? Settle down for a warm tub bath. Was this just a bad day? Or is something inside you calling out for meaning, for a deeper reality than what you find every day on that television or computer screen of yours? Talk it over with a friend. Is it time to re-examine your career goals? Are there loose ends that need to be tied up? Is there a nagging feeling that you need to be forgiven for something you've done? Do you just need a good night's sleep? Or are you being called to pilgrimage?

  You will know it is a call if the urge becomes a longing and if that longing stays with you for more than a day or two. Once you hear the call, you heed it by giving shape to the pilgrimage experience – determine time frames and possible destinations.
- Determine if your pilgrimage requires you to "get away." If it does, pull out your personal pilgrimage templates and index, and decide where you will go and who might guide you. A place may come to mind instantly. If not, try exploring local bookstores in the days that follow; look for city guides or books

like *Afoot and Afield,* which document local hikes and walks. Call friends and family for suggestions. Check out newspapers, chambers of commerce, county maps – all may have clues about your destination.

- Identify an appropriate two-day period for your pilgrimage. Put it in your daily planner the same way you would a gym workout or an important business meeting. Remember not to put anything else there for The Night Before, the day of The Journey, or the night of The Homecoming. When people remind you of groceries you're supposed to pick up that weekend or of committee meetings you're supposed to attend, let them know you'll be unavailable during those days to everyone but yourself.
- Ask for blessings from a family member, clergy, friend, or group. With a personal pilgrimage, all you have to do is explain your intention – "I need to take a couple of days for myself this weekend," or "You keep telling me to *chill*, so I'm going to take some long walks and do some thinking over the next few days." You can end with, "Can I get your blessing?" or "Would you wish me luck?" A simple nod is all you really need to be blessed.

II. THE NIGHT BEFORE

To cross the threshold from this time and place to another, you engage in pilgrimage rituals that prepare your heart and soul for your sacred journey.

- Pack your pilgrim's satchel. It's important to be organized so that you feel relaxed and ready for whatever comes your way. The templates will guide you on what to pack. Don't forget the directions to your destination and your copy of *Personal Pilgrimage at Midlife.*
- Prepare a meditative space with candles, incense, music, and any other sensual aids that will help you downshift from postmodern fast-tracker to postmodern pilgrim. By the way, you may need none of the above. Perhaps the best gift you will give yourself on your pilgrimage is space for silence and emptiness. Try it.

Altars I have known and loved

My friend Patty recently invited me and several of her girlfriends for an altar-building party at her home. She liked the altar I have in my own home and decided this would be a good thing for her to have as well.

My altar is simply a long table situated against one wall of my living room and on which I place a few personal objects: some stones I found in the Puget Sound while on a particularly exciting Outward Bound experience, a black velvet box given to me by a friend, a crystal also given to me by a friend, a sweet little Buddha statue which was a Christmas present from my daughter, a blue bottle of natural fragrances mixed for me by my friend Debbie, and two pictures of beloved cats who left me for the wilds. These objects are arranged on a square piece of lace and remind me

- Engage in your own meditation practices. While the templates will suggest certain writing and meditative exercises, they will also suggest that you use the practices with which you are comfortable. Use chanting, singing, praying, meditating, visualizing, deep breathing, stretching, yoga, or anything else that helps you focus and go inward. You might even use new meditative techniques, if you've discovered any you would like to try.
- Become familiar with your inspirational guide. The templates will assist you by asking you to think about your guide's life, and to integrate his or her insights into your pilgrimage. Read the mini-biography provided and any other notes you might have prepared yourself. Use your imagination to draw close to your guide and concentrate on his or her words of wisdom.
- Journal in your copy of *Personal Pilgrimage at Midlife*, or in any other journal you keep. Remember that the questions are designed to help you focus, to give you a starting point for your contemplative experience; they are only suggestions.

every day of the special people in my life and of my love of things spiritual.

I fashioned my own altar after that of a yoga instructor I visited once. Her altar was strewn with photographs of family and spiritual masters, and with stones and dried flowers. It was the first time I had ever seen a home altar. After seeing hers, I eagerly began to think about how to create my own.

Patty's altar is a long piece of plywood painted black. We propped it up on beautiful decorative bricks, and each of us placed a special object on it. In the center of the altar, Patty placed a beautiful three-wick candle. She constantly takes things from her altar and gives them away to her friends and family. She adds things to her altar, as well. It is a living work.

If you would like to create a sacred space in your own home, you might try Peg Streep's book *Altars Made Easy.* Be creative. A particularly interesting home altar I once encountered was a huge canvas placed horizontally in the center of an artist's living room, where she scripted a different word on its surface every morning, such as *Love* or *Creativity.* Create something that reflects you and those things you love and revere.

III. THE JOURNEY

With great anticipation you awaken to your pilgrimage day. To assure blessed passage, you do the following. (See suggestions for activities page 73.)

- Engage in your own meditation practices before starting out and journal before you depart, in order to focus and prepare.
- Arrive at your destination. Experience the place and the moment, the stretch of time you have carved out for yourself. Reflect on whatever questions and issues seem most important to you. Journal. Be entirely present. Note all the details and experience as deeply as possible the sense of the place you have chosen. Note the lay of the land – every shadow and play of light. Pay

attention to the weight of the air. The texture of the sky above. Be especially aware of the feeling of sacredness that may surround the space simply because you have chosen it as a destination for your own heart and soul.

- Leave a gift in the name of your inspirational guide, at the shrine of your deeper reality. Remember to do this only if it will not detract from the natural state of the site as you found it.
  Leave behind a coin to signify your presence as a postmodern pilgrim.

IV. THE HOMECOMING

Your journey is done. It is the night of your homecoming. You have come full circle. Now it's time to recross the threshold back to your everyday life.

- Engage in your own meditation practices and ritual ceremonies. Feast on delectable foods, steam yourself with hot towels, fill vases with exquisite flora. Celebrate!
- Reflect on what your journey has wrought. Write in the journal sections of this book and communicate with your inspirational guide, with friends, with your God, revealing the treasures you collected on your pilgrimage with great humility. As you engage in these activities, you begin to think about how the pilgrimage experience and all it has brought forth can be integrated into your daily life. With a pilgrimage, the lessons are real and they are now. While you may have snapshots to commemorate your experience, the pilgrimage is not frozen in time. The experience and all it had to give are part of you now. That is the way with pilgrimage.

A final word

Though there are 12 travel templates in this book, you don't have to take a personal pilgrimage every month. Maybe you want to take one every other month, or even once a year. This book will hold you, in that case, well into your midlife journey.

Blessings.

Activities

In addition to the journaling you will do during your personal pilgrimage, you might want to incorporate activities that will make your journey even more meaningful. Perhaps you'll want to select one activity for each travel template.

1. Photograph your journey. Take your camera with you on your personal pilgrimage and take pictures of the places and things you encounter. Pay special attention to the way you photograph things and ask yourself what you want to capture. Drop the photos off at a developing place before you come home. Once you are home, decide how you will use the best photos from your journey. Will you take one of them to work and place it on your bulletin board? Will you turn it into a special postcard for someone? Will you post it on your website or send it via e-mail to your friends? Think of creative ways to share your photographs.

2. Correspondence. Use nice stationery and a favorite pen to write letters to your inspirational guide, your internal guide, your Higher Power, your mom, or to friends and departed loved ones. Think about mailing the letter with only the name of the person in the address spot on the envelope.

3. Post cards. Buy some beautiful post cards and take them with you on your journey. Decide who you would like to connect to during your journey, and write post cards while you are at your sacred site. Mail them on the way home.

4. Sketches. Whether you're an artist or not, take this opportunity to pull out or buy a sketch pad and pastels, or color crayons or charcoal, and draw to your heart's content, not worrying about whether your artwork is worthy or good, thinking only about the process of drawing and expressing yourself. Try drawing a picture of your Higher Power, your internal guide, your inspirational guide, your sacred site, or objects you find at your sacred site. Decide what you'll do with your sketch when you return from your journey. Would you like to make it part of an evening ritual – fold it up and place it over a beautiful flame, releasing its energy fully into the universe? Or send it off to someone who would appreciate it? Or put it in a special box?

5. Collage. If you like to cut and paste, gather a collection of magazines and flip through them, searching for images that represent your search for today. What do you think you're looking for? What might you find? Clip images that catch your eye and paste them on some cardboard for later reference.

6. Write a poem. You may not be a poet, or a writer of any kind, and remember, you don't have to rhyme to be a good poet. Try writing freestyle adjectives about how you feel, maybe a few sentence fragments about what this experience means to you, some symbols that express midlife for you. Put it all together and you have a poem.

7. Magnify. Find a pair of binoculars and use them to magnify your beautiful surroundings. Be careful you don't appear to be spying! The binoculars will give you a different perspective on what you're seeing and will serve as a consciousness shifter.

8. Heart talks. When you reach out for a blessing from a friend or colleague, ask for a few minutes to talk about what's in your heart. Hear yourself talk about your journey and make sure it is real for both you and those around you.

9. Yoga. To be receptive on your journey, it will be helpful to release all tension from your body and there is no better path for that than yoga. Yoga is a work-in, not a workout. It stretches the muscles so that you can let go of stress, freeing your internal pathways from clutter and obstacles. If you aren't familiar with yoga, just try some gentle stretching exercises, lying on the floor, sitting up and standing. Be very gentle. And don't forget to breathe.

10. E-mail alert. Send out an alert to your best friends, informing them that you are off on a soul journey, receptive to all kinds of questions and answers. Alert them when you return, as well.

11. Deep breathing. As valuable as yoga, in terms of stress relief, is deep breathing. Do it purposefully and lovingly. Breathe in beautiful fragrances, breathe out gorgeous colors. Breathe in light, breathe out coolness or warmth. Be conscious about your breath and try staying with it for a significant period of time.

12. Personalpilgrimage.net. Write up your personal pilgrimage experience and send it to www.personalpilgrimage.net, where it will be posted for all to see at some future date. Don't forget to include a photo.

Ambience

The ambience you desire for the night before your pilgrimage, and for your homecoming, can be created. Experiment with the following:

- Lights – candle effects, colored light bulbs, scarves thrown over lamps, no light, one dim light, starlight, natural dusk light.
- Fragrance – flowers such as the jasmine and the rose, incense, sage, scented candles, potpourri, drops of scented oil, hickory logs in the fireplace, a pot of stew in the crock pot.
- Music – any kind, from Gregorian chants to country western. Try making your own; pull out that dusty guitar or experiment with a new drum.
- Silence – turn off the phone, the CD player, and the clock chimes. Send the kids on an overnight and the husband to a football game. Lock the dog in his room. Contemplate the beauty of emptiness.
- Dance – sway or stomp, try different forms of ethnic music, tell a story with your hand movements, pretend you are dancing for your Higher Power, dance with yourself in front of a mirror.
- Color – pay attention to the colors that already exist in the room around you, fill the room with multi-colored bouquets, develop a color theme and find objects of that color to surround yourself with, throw colored scarves over lamps.
- Arrangement – arrange furniture and objects in ways that enhance or shift your mood. You may want to unclutter the room before you begin your Night Before ceremony. On the other hand, you might want to clutter it up for some reason! Get in touch with your needs.
- Forms – surround yourself with forms that are significant for you. Circles, triangles, arrows, or hearts. Cut them out of paper, draw them on flip charts.

PART 2

PERSONAL PILGRIMAGE TEMPLATES

Career Paths

Career

If you are a midlifer examining your life's work, consider taking your questions to a place that for you symbolizes pathways. Whether you actually walk a path on this pilgrimage or sit quietly in view of one, whether you bring a picture of a walkway with you for contemplation, or draw your own picture, think of your career as one of many paths within your life. Think about the one you have chosen, and what career paths you might be drawn to traverse now.

Prayer, Meditation, or Affirmation for your Career Paths journey:

The outward work can never be small if the inward one is great,
and the outward work can never be great or good
if the inward one is small or of little worth.

MEISTER ECKHART, TRANSLATED BY MATTHEW FOX

Date of your personal pilgrimage

HEEDING THE CALL

What called you to this pilgrimage – what questions, what struggles, what events, what people, what challenges?

If you decide to have an inspirational guide on this journey, who will it be?

Why?

Who will bless your journey? (Call him or her before you go.)

THE NIGHT BEFORE

Preparing your space

What ambience do you wish to create and how will you create it? (See page 74 for ideas.)

What rituals or ceremonies might you engage in? (See page 66 for ideas.)

What music will you make or listen to?

Preparing your heart and mind

Start your reading and contemplation with a prayer, meditation, or affirmation. You may wish to use the one at the beginning of this travel template.

Review pages 26 to 29 in this book and select several or all of the questions listed in that section of the book for journaling. The questions are listed below for easy access. Underline the ones you want to contemplate during your journey tomorrow.

1. What is work?
2. What does it mean to be called?
3. What had you learned about career by the time you were 8? 18? 28? What have you learned about career, sum total, today?
4. What did you like to do best when you were five years old?
5. What do you think your purpose or mission is?
6. What would you do with your life if money were no object?
7. How would you like your eulogy to read?
8. What advice would you give future generations about work and career?
9. Would you have done anything differently with your early career, if you knew what you know today?
10. What do you need to do to make your life more fulfilling as you make "the gentle turn"?

You might also want to answer the following questions: How do the life and wisdom of my inspirational guide speak to these questions?

Work-life balance solutions

At a recent speaking engagement, I asked a roomful of human resource professionals what their companies might be doing to assure balance for employees. Though some audience members reported that work-life balance benefits were sadly lacking in their companies, most contributed interesting corporate solutions to the challenges of juggling work and life. Many reported innovative solutions, such as

- on-site stress counselors
- personal bookkeepers
- flexible work schedules
- errand-running services.

These are excellent and valid life balance offerings from companies who are concerned about employee health and productivity. But at a recent corporate conference where he was the keynote speaker, Bill Taylor, co-founder of *Fast Company* magazine, suggested yet another perspective – one that focuses on inward solutions. Taylor told his audience that companies who thrive today will be those who are not only constantly innovating and moving

What do I really want to know?

Travel details

Check list: You have

- ❍ directions to your destination
- ❍ water and snacks
- ❍ your copy of *Personal Pilgrimage at Midlife*
- ❍ a pen or pencil
- ❍ a gift and token to leave behind
- ❍ a blessing from someone
- ❍ an idea of how you will celebrate your homecoming (See page 72 for ideas.)

Saying goodnight

End your evening with a prayer, meditation, or affirmation. You may wish to use the one at the beginning of this travel template.

forward, but also those that take time to "slow down, refresh and recharge" – not just because it's good for the individual, he said, but also because "it's in those moments of quiet reflection that you're going to come up with the next set of great ideas that will put you ahead of the competition."

Here are things some companies are doing to encourage quite reflection:

- creating quiet zones and meditation rooms on-site
- providing creativity workshops referred to as "vision quests"
- holding "values" discussions regularly throughout the year
- providing yoga classes
- building garden walkways with meditation spots around facilities

THE JOURNEY

Begin your day with a prayer, mediation, or affirmation.
You may wish to use the one at the beginning of this travel template.

Reminder:
Don't forget your pilgrim's satchel with book, pen, directions, water and snacks.

When you arrive at your destination, take time to
- breathe deeply
- pay attention to the details in your surroundings
- touch things around you.

Things you may wish to contemplate
- a Higher Power
- the life and words of your inspirational guide
- all that you have to be grateful for
- the wonders of your life
- your unique challenges.

Journal from your heart, considering the life and wisdom of your inspirational guide, and answering some of the questions you selected from this book the night before.

Leave your gift and token in a special place.
You may decide to leave the gift somewhere else, on the way home.
End with a prayer, meditation, or affirmation.
You may wish to use the one at the beginning of this travel template.

THE HOMECOMING

Prepare your homecoming space, prepare your heart, and contemplate these questions:

> What did you learn from your personal pilgrimage today?
> How will you integrate what you learned into your daily life?
> What questions will you live in, during the days ahead?

Journal from your heart.

End with a prayer, meditation, or affirmation.
You may wish to use the one at the beginning of this travel template.

Mortal's Portals

Mortality

If, like many in the middle years, you are coming to grips with one of Western society's least favorite subjects – death – you may wish to deal with it by sitting near a door: a beautifully carved museum door, a church door, the door to your backyard or perhaps a gateway, such as one that opens onto a garden or a yard, or an archway leading to another space. At some point on your pilgrimage, pass through the door.

Prayer, Meditation, or Affirmation for your Mortal's Portals journey:

It is very beautiful over there…

THOMAS EDISON'S DYING WORDS

Date of your personal pilgrimage

HEEDING THE CALL

What called you to this pilgrimage – what questions, what struggles, what events, what people, what challenges?

If you decide to have an inspirational guide on this journey, who will it be?

Why?

Who will bless your journey? (Call him or her before you go.)

THE NIGHT BEFORE

Preparing your space

What ambience do you wish to create and how will you create it? (See page 74 for ideas.)

What rituals or ceremonies might you engage in? (See page 66 for ideas.)

What music will you make or listen to?

Preparing your heart and mind

Start your reading and contemplation with a prayer, meditation, or affirmation. You may wish to use the one at the beginning of this travel template. Review pages 29 to 33 in this book and select several or all of the questions listed in that section of the book for journaling. The questions are listed below for easy access. Underline the ones you want to contemplate during your journey tomorrow.

1. What is death?
2. Why do we fear death?
3. What will sustain you through death?
4. What had you learned about death by the time you were 8? 18? 28?
5. When we die, do our souls live on?
6. Are we in a constant decline toward death?
7. Are you ready to die?
8. How have others who have died made an impact on your life?
9. How are life and death alike?
10. What do you need to do to accept your mortality?

You might also want to answer the following questions: How do the life and wisdom of my inspirational guide speak to these questions?

What do I really want to know?

Travel details

Check list: You have

- ❍ directions to your destination
- ❍ water and snacks
- ❍ your copy of *Personal Pilgrimage at Midlife*
- ❍ a pen or pencil
- ❍ a gift and token to leave behind
- ❍ a blessing from someone
- ❍ an idea of how you will celebrate your homecoming (See page 72 for ideas.)

Saying goodnight

End your evening with a prayer, meditation, or affirmation.
You may wish to use the one at the beginning of this travel template.

Reminder:
Don't forget your pilgrim's satchel with book, pen, directions, water and snacks.

THE JOURNEY

Begin your day with a prayer, mediation, or affirmation. You may wish to use the one at the beginning of this travel template.

When you arrive at your destination, take time to

- breathe deeply
- pay attention to the details in your surroundings
- touch things around you.

Things you may wish to contemplate

- a Higher Power
- the life and words of your inspirational guide
- all that you have to be grateful for
- the wonders of your life
- your unique challenges.

Journal from your heart, considering the life and wisdom of your inspirational guide, and answering some of the questions you selected from this book the night before.

The mysteries of caves

While all forms of nature – from trees to rocks to streams – have been revered as sacred at one time or another, the earliest known sacred places are naturally formed caves. Lascaux in France is the best example of a cave imbued with sacred qualities. Within the protective walls of this cave, prehistoric humans lived, ate, and recorded their activities and cycles, celebrated and ritualized their lives.

Because the earth has been referred to in female terms, the cave has been identified as the womb of Mother Earth. The cave may protect. But it may also imprison and entrap. These ambiguities, along with the deep, dark, and sometimes dangerous qualities of caves, add to their aura of the sacred and the mysterious.

Leave your gift and token in a special place.
You may decide to leave the gift somewhere else, on the way home.
End with a prayer, meditation, or affirmation.
You may wish to use the one at the beginning of this travel template.

THE HOMECOMING

Prepare your homecoming space, prepare your heart, and contemplate these questions:

What did you learn from your personal pilgrimage today?
How will you integrate what you learned into your daily life?
What questions will you live in, during the days ahead?

Journal from your heart.

End with a prayer, meditation, or affirmation.
You may wish to use the one at the beginning of this travel template.

Water's Edge

Sexual identity

Water has an ancient tie to sexuality in dream archetypes and in the symbolism of ancient cultures. For a pilgrimage to the depths of yourself, go to water's edge and ask questions about your sexuality. Perhaps there is a natural body of water nearby where you can step to the edge and look in. If you are near an ocean, maybe the waves will crash their answers on your shores. Or maybe there is an exquisite fountain somewhere downtown, maybe somewhere on your own premises. Let the water reflect the answers within.

Prayer, Meditation, or Affirmation for your journey to Water's Edge:

I am exploring my deepest thoughts about my deepest self.
What do I find?

Date of your personal pilgrimage

___

HEEDING THE CALL

What called you to this pilgrimage – what questions, what struggles, what events, what people, what challenges?

___

___

___

If you decide to have an inspirational guide on this journey, who will it be?

___

Why?

Who will bless your journey? (Call him or her before you go.)

THE NIGHT BEFORE

Preparing your space

What ambience do you wish to create and how will you create it? (See page 74 for ideas.)

What rituals or ceremonies might you engage in? (See page 66 for ideas.)

What music will you make or listen to?

Preparing your heart and mind

Start your reading and contemplation with a prayer, meditation, or affirmation. You may wish to use the one at the beginning of this travel template.

Review pages 33 to 36 in this book and select several or all of the questions listed in that section of the book for journaling. The questions are listed below for easy access. Underline the ones you want to contemplate during your journey tomorrow.

1. What role has religion played in shaping your sexual identity?
2. What roles have culture, personal history, and biology played in shaping your sexual identity?
3. How would you describe your sexual identity? Find some adjectives.
4. What role do you want sex to play in your life today?
5. What is sexy to you?
6. What do you value about sexual activity? What do you fear?
7. What had you learned about sex by the time you were 8? 18? 28?
8. How does your body perception affect your attitudes about sex?
9. What advice do you have for future generations about sex?
10. If it weren't for sex…

You might also want to answer the following questions: How do the life and wisdom of my inspirational guide speak to these questions?

What do I really want to know?

Travel details

Check list: You have

- ❍ directions to your destination
- ❍ water and snacks
- ❍ your copy of *Personal Pilgrimage at Midlife*
- ❍ a pen or pencil
- ❍ a gift and token to leave behind
- ❍ a blessing from someone
- ❍ an idea of how you will celebrate your homecoming (See page 72 for ideas.)

Saying goodnight

End your evening with a prayer, meditation, or affirmation. You may wish to use the one at the beginning of this travel template.

Reminder:

Don't forget your pilgrim's satchel with book, pen, directions, water and snacks.

THE JOURNEY

Begin your day with a prayer, mediation, or affirmation. You may wish to use the one at the beginning of this travel template.

When you arrive at your destination, take time to

- breathe deeply
- pay attention to the details in your surroundings
- touch things around you.

Things you may wish to contemplate

- a Higher Power
- the life and words of your inspirational guide
- all that you have to be grateful for
- the wonders of your life
- your unique challenges.

Journal from your heart, considering the life and wisdom of your inspirational guide, and answering some of the questions you selected from this book the night before.

Water symbols

Besides being a symbol for sexuality in dreams, water is an ancient religious symbol for creation and for life. In fact, many religions assert that water is the primordial element from which life springs. Sacred Hindu text reveals that all beings emerged from the sea. In the Judeo-Christian tradition, scripture describes the spirit of God stirring on the waters before he creates a firmament to divide them. The Koran states that all living things were created from water.

Various religions and cultures have used water as a holy sacrament. Ancient Greeks enshrined sacred springs, erecting elaborate, artificial basins and surrounding them with icons of deities. Christians recognize its innate spiritual qualities, using it to baptize – to impart spiritual life. In India, the sacred Ganges frees the bather from sin.

Through the ages, water has been imbued with healing qualities. Today, more than six million people trek to Lourdes, France, each year, where in the mid-19th century, Bernadette's vision of the Virgin Mary resulted in the discovery of a perennial spring of miraculous, healing water. Today, it is not only the jogger and the athlete who carry around bottles of spring water for health, the average person (I for one) also sees the significance of water as an everyday, healing, life-giving substance.

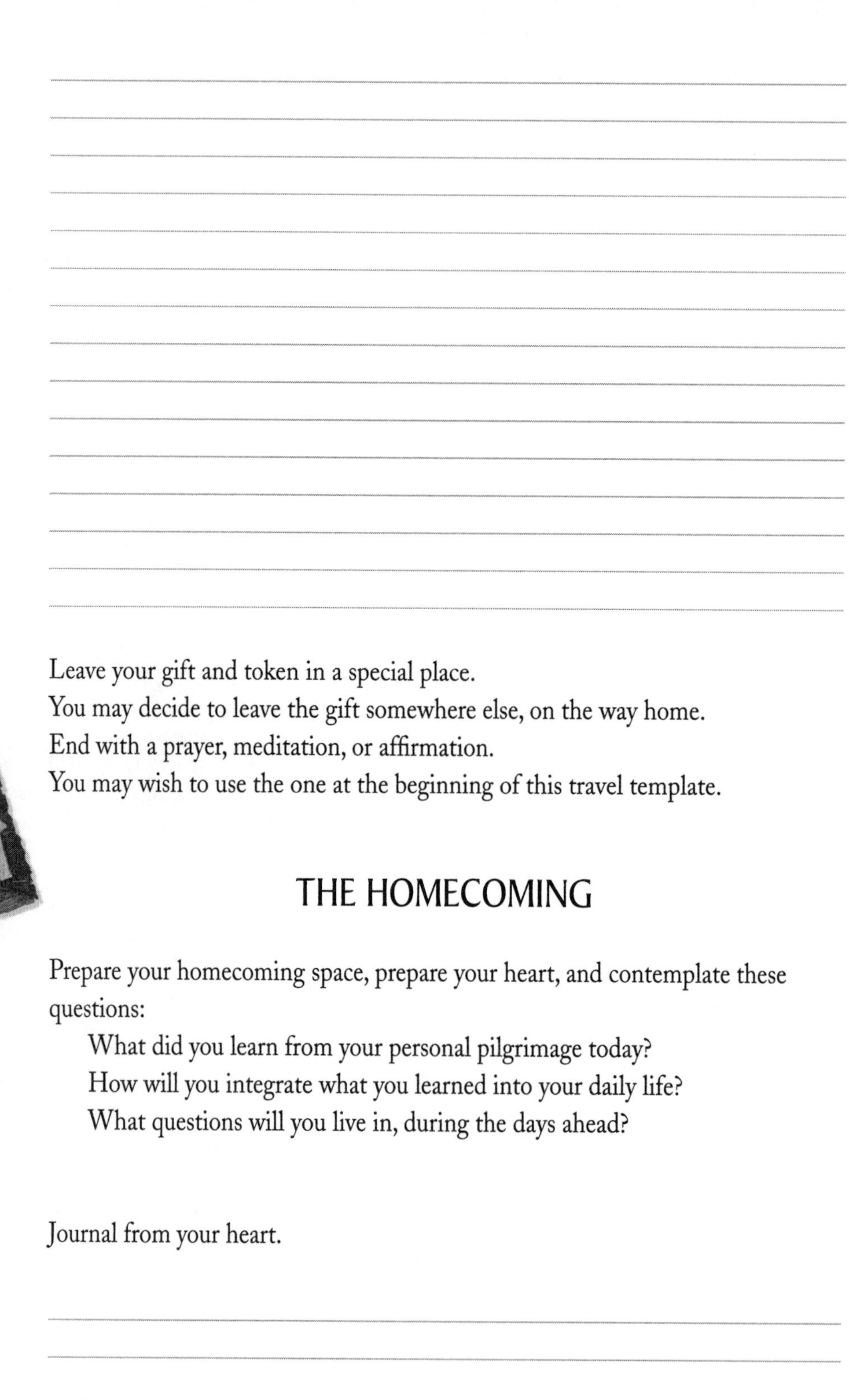

Leave your gift and token in a special place.
You may decide to leave the gift somewhere else, on the way home.
End with a prayer, meditation, or affirmation.
You may wish to use the one at the beginning of this travel template.

THE HOMECOMING

Prepare your homecoming space, prepare your heart, and contemplate these questions:

What did you learn from your personal pilgrimage today?
How will you integrate what you learned into your daily life?
What questions will you live in, during the days ahead?

Journal from your heart.

End with a prayer, meditation, or affirmation.
You may wish to use the one at the beginning of this travel template.

Sacred Temple

Body Awareness

Some say the body is a temple for your soul. Whether you have never set foot in a church, or whether you attend a temple service every week, take yourself now to a sacred place of worship and contemplate your one and only body. Try a small chapel. Or a huge sanctuary. Try going to a church you never would have thought of attending before. If you go during a time when a formal service is taking place, be especially aware of the space you are sitting in, the ears you are listening with, the eyes you are seeing with. If you choose to go on a day when the rooms or yards are empty, find a particularly quiet space where you can listen to what your body has to say.

Prayer, Meditation, or Affirmation for your Sacred Temple journey:

If anything is sacred, the human body is sacred.

WALT WHITMAN

Date of your personal pilgrimage

HEEDING THE CALL

What called you to this pilgrimage – what questions, what struggles, what events, what people, what challenges?

If you decide to have an inspirational guide on this journey, who will it be?

Why?

Who will bless your journey? (Call him or her before you go.)

THE NIGHT BEFORE

Preparing your space

What ambience do you wish to create and how will you create it? (See page 74 for ideas.)

What rituals or ceremonies might you engage in? (See page 66 for ideas.)

What music will you make or listen to?

Preparing your heart and mind

Start your reading and contemplation with a prayer, meditation, or affirmation. You may wish to use the one at the beginning of this travel template.

Review pages 36 to 40 in this book and select several or all of the questions listed in that section of the book for journaling. The questions are listed below for easy access. Underline the ones you want to contemplate during your journey tomorrow.

1. How has your body been a friend to you throughout your life?
2. How has your body been less than a friend?
3. How do you view your relationship with your body today?
4. How has your body changed since you were 8? 18? 28?
5. What do you love most about your body?
6. Are you always aware of your body?
7. How do you thank your body?
8. How do you think others perceive your body? Is that important to you?
9. If your body were to say something to you now, what would it say?
10. What part of your body do you love most? What part do you love least? How can you integrate the part you love most with the part you love least?

You might also want to answer the following questions: How do the life and wisdom of my inspirational guide speak to these questions?

What do I really want to know?

Travel details

Check list: You have

- ❍ directions to your destination
- ❍ water and snacks
- ❍ your copy of *Personal Pilgrimage at Midlife*
- ❍ a pen or pencil
- ❍ a gift and token to leave behind
- ❍ a blessing from someone
- ❍ an idea of how you will celebrate your homecoming (See page 72 for ideas.)

Saying goodnight

End your evening with a prayer, meditation, or affirmation. You may wish to use the one at the beginning of this travel template.

THE JOURNEY

Begin your day with a prayer, mediation, or affirmation. You may wish to use the one at the beginning of this travel template.

When you arrive at your destination, take time to

- breathe deeply
- pay attention to the details in your surroundings
- touch things around you.

Reminder:
Don't forget your pilgrim's satchel with book, pen, directions, water and snacks.

Things you may wish to contemplate

- a Higher Power
- the life and words of your inspirational guide
- all that you have to be grateful for
- the wonders of your life
- your unique challenges.

Journal from your heart, considering the life and wisdom of your inspirational guide, and answering some of the questions you selected from this book the night before.

Leave your gift and token in a special place.
You may decide to leave the gift somewhere else, on the way home.
End with a prayer, meditation, or affirmation.
You may wish to use the one at the beginning of this travel template.

THE HOMECOMING

Prepare your homecoming space, prepare your heart, and contemplate these questions:

What did you learn from your personal pilgrimage today?
How will you integrate what you learned into your daily life?
What questions will you live in, during the days ahead?

Journal from your heart.

End with a prayer, meditation, or affirmation.

You may wish to use the one at the beginning of this travel template.

Evergreen

Generativity/legacy

To contemplate how we do live on, forever, despite our mortality, you might wish to find someplace very green – either indoors or outdoors – and contemplate your legacy. Rolling hills, lawns, gardens, nurseries, botanical sanctuaries, forests… Find a pine somewhere, and ask yourself what legacy it has left.

Prayer, Meditation, or Affirmation for your Evergreen journey:

You may forget but
let me tell you
this: someone in
some future time
will think of us.

Sappho

Date of your personal pilgrimage

HEEDING THE CALL

What called you to this pilgrimage – what questions, what struggles, what events, what people, what challenges?

If you decide to have an inspirational guide on this journey, who will it be?

Why?

Who will bless your journey? (Call him or her before you go.)

THE NIGHT BEFORE

Preparing your space

What ambience do you wish to create and how will you create it? (See page 74 for ideas.)

What rituals or ceremonies might you engage in? (See page 66 for ideas.)

What music will you make or listen to?

Preparing your heart and mind

Start your reading and contemplation with a prayer, meditation, or affirmation. You may wish to use the one at the beginning of this travel template.

Review pages 40 to 43 in this book and select several or all of the questions listed in that section of the book for journaling. The questions are listed below for easy access. Underline the ones you want to contemplate during your journey tomorrow.

1. What is your purpose? How are you fulfilling it?
2. What gifts have you received from others throughout your life?
3. What gifts have you given others?
4. What legacies have been most important to you in your life?
5. What three adjectives would describe how you want to be remembered?
6. What three important things would you like mentioned in your eulogy?
7. How will your presence on earth make a difference in the lives of your family and friends, after you are gone?
8. What things can you do now to establish your legacy?
9. How are you contributing to the earth's supporting ecosystem?
10. What is left to accomplish, before you go?

You might also want to answer the following questions: How do the life and wisdom of my inspirational guide speak to these questions?

What do I really want to know?

Travel details

Check list: You have

- ❍ directions to your destination
- ❍ water and snacks
- ❍ your copy of *Personal Pilgrimage at Midlife*
- ❍ a pen or pencil
- ❍ a gift and token to leave behind
- ❍ a blessing from someone
- ❍ an idea of how you will celebrate your homecoming
  (See page 72 for ideas.)

Saying goodnight

End your evening with a prayer, meditation, or affirmation. You may wish to use the one at the beginning of this travel template.

THE JOURNEY

Begin your day with a prayer, mediation, or affirmation. You may wish to use the one at the beginning of this travel template.

Reminder:
Don't forget your pilgrim's satchel with book, pen, directions, water and snacks.

When you arrive at your destination, take time to

- breathe deeply
- pay attention to the details in your surroundings
- touch things around you.

Things you may wish to contemplate

- a Higher Power
- the life and words of your inspirational guide
- all that you have to be grateful for
- the wonders of your life
- your unique challenges.

Journal from your heart, considering the life and wisdom of your inspirational guide, and answering some of the questions you selected from this book the night before.

Leave your gift and token in a special place.
You may decide to leave the gift somewhere else, on the way home.
End with a prayer, meditation, or affirmation.
You may wish to use the one at the beginning of this travel template.

THE HOMECOMING

Prepare your homecoming space, prepare your heart, and contemplate these questions:

What did you learn from your personal pilgrimage today?
How will you integrate what you learned into your daily life?
What questions will you live in, during the days ahead?

Journal from your heart.

End with a prayer, meditation, or affirmation.
You may wish to use the one at the beginning of this travel template.

Watchtower

Spirituality

Is your spirit separate from your body? Or is it inextricably connected? An ancient question, to be sure. One way to tell is to take yourself to a crowded spot and watch the masses walk by. Maybe you'd like to pilgrimage to the airport, to the zoo, to a downtown shopping mall or busy street. Stand in the background and crowd-watch. Do you see individual spirits in the faces of passers-by? Do you see a collective spirit? Are you spirit, watching spirit? What do you see or feel from your watchtower?

Prayer, Meditation, or Affirmation for your Watchtower journey:

We are not human beings having a spiritual experience.
We are spiritual beings having a human experience.

TEILHARD DE CHARDIN

Date of your personal pilgrimage

HEEDING THE CALL

What called you to this pilgrimage – what questions, what struggles, what events, what people, what challenges?

If you decide to have an inspirational guide on this journey, who will it be?

Why?

Who will bless your journey? (Call him or her before you go.)

THE NIGHT BEFORE

Preparing your space

What ambience do you wish to create and how will you create it? (See page 74 for ideas.)

What rituals or ceremonies might you engage in? (See page 66 for ideas.)

What music will you make or listen to?

Preparing your heart and mind

Start your reading and contemplation with a prayer, meditation, or affirmation. You may wish to use the one at the beginning of this travel template.

Review pages 43 to 45 in this book and select several or all of the questions listed in that section of the book for journaling. The questions are listed below for easy access. Underline the ones you want to contemplate during your journey tomorrow.

1. What is spirit?
2. What adjectives would you use to describe your spirit?
3. Where is your spirit?
4. How long have you known your spirit?
5. What other spirits are close to you? What adjectives would you use to describe each of them?
6. What is important – body, mind, spirit, or heart? Why?
7. How do you nurture your spirit today?
8. What does your spirit need?
9. Has your spirit changed since you were 8? 18? 28? If so, how?
10. Where did your spirit come from?

You might also want to answer the following questions: How do the life and wisdom of my inspirational guide speak to these questions?

What do I really want to know?

Travel details

Check list: You have

- ❍ directions to your destination
- ❍ water and snacks
- ❍ your copy of *Personal Pilgrimage at Midlife*
- ❍ a pen or pencil
- ❍ a gift and token to leave behind
- ❍ a blessing from someone
- ❍ an idea of how you will celebrate your homecoming (See page 72 for ideas.)

Saying goodnight

End your evening with a prayer, meditation, or affirmation. You may wish to use the one at the beginning of this travel template.

THE JOURNEY

Begin your day with a prayer, mediation, or affirmation. You may wish to use the one at the beginning of this travel template.

Reminder:
Don't forget your pilgrim's satchel with book, pen, directions, water and snacks.

When you arrive at your destination, take time to

- breathe deeply
- pay attention to the details in your surroundings
- touch things around you.

Things you may wish to contemplate

- a Higher Power
- the life and words of your inspirational guide
- all that you have to be grateful for
- the wonders of your life
- your unique challenges.

Journal from your heart, considering the life and wisdom of your inspirational guide, and answering some of the questions you selected from this book the night before.

Leave your gift and token in a special place.
You may decide to leave the gift somewhere else, on the way home.
End with a prayer, meditation, or affirmation.
You may wish to use the one at the beginning of this travel template.

THE HOMECOMING

Prepare your homecoming space, prepare your heart, and contemplate these questions:

What did you learn from your personal pilgrimage today?
How will you integrate what you learned into your daily life?
What questions will you live in, during the days ahead?

Journal from your heart.

End with a prayer, meditation, or affirmation.
You may wish to use the one at the beginning of this travel template.

Abundance Point

Finances

If you can think of your finances as the path to material abundance rather than as the source of your poverty, it may free you up from anxiety and stress. If you can truly realize that money does not buy happiness and that material abundance is not the only form of abundance, you may find a deep and lasting peace. Maybe you have already liberated yourself by thinking about money as the source of your material abundance and maybe you are ready to explore the concept of spiritual abundance further. Maybe you have never been at peace with your relationship with money and need to identify ways to improve it. Whatever your current condition, now is the time to take stock of your finances. Find a place that for you symbolizes abundance. Flower fields? A grove or forest? The lemon tree in your back yard that rains lemons every year? Make that place your abundance point and pilgrimage there.

Prayer, Meditation, or Affirmation for your journey to Abundance Point:

The road to financial freedom begins not in a bank
or even in a financial planner's office, but in your head.

SUZE ORMAN, THE 9 STEPS TO FINANCIAL FREEDOM

Date of your personal pilgrimage

HEEDING THE CALL

What called you to this pilgrimage – what questions, what struggles, what events, what people, what challenges?

If you decide to have an inspirational guide on this journey, who will it be?

Why?

Who will bless your journey? (Call him or her before you go.)

THE NIGHT BEFORE

Preparing your space

What ambience do you wish to create and how will you create it? (See page 74 for ideas.)

What rituals or ceremonies might you engage in? (See page 66 for ideas.)

What music will you make or listen to?______________________________

____

____

Preparing your heart and mind

Start your reading and contemplation with a prayer, meditation, or affirmation. You may wish to use the one at the beginning of this travel template.

Review pages 45 to 48 in this book and select several or all of the questions listed in that section of the book for journaling. The questions are listed below for easy access. Underline the ones you want to contemplate during your journey tomorrow.

1. What has money given you in your lifetime thus far?
2. How is money your best friend?
3. Has money ever betrayed you? When?
4. What adjectives would you use to describe your relationship with money when you were 8? 18? 28? Today?
5. What adjectives best describe the state of your finances today?
6. How would you change your financial situation?
7. If you didn't need the money and possessions you have today, what would you do with them?
8. When are you most aware of the flow and energy that money represents? How can you bring that awareness to your daily events?
9. What do you need to do to put your financial matters in order?
10. How will finances be part of your legacy?

You might also want to answer the following questions: How do the life and wisdom of my inspirational guide speak to these questions?

____

____

What do I really want to know?

____

____

Travel details

Check list: You have

- ❍ directions to your destination
- ❍ water and snacks
- ❍ your copy of *Personal Pilgrimage at Midlife*
- ❍ a pen or pencil
- ❍ a gift and token to leave behind
- ❍ a blessing from someone
- ❍ an idea of how you will celebrate your homecoming (See page 72 for ideas.)

Saying goodnight

End your evening with a prayer, meditation, or affirmation. You may wish to use the one at the beginning of this travel template.

THE JOURNEY

Begin your day with a prayer, mediation, or affirmation. You may wish to use the one at the beginning of this travel template.

Reminder:
Don't forget your pilgrim's satchel with book, pen, directions, water and snacks.

When you arrive at your destination, take time to

- breathe deeply
- pay attention to the details in your surroundings
- touch things around you.

Things you may wish to contemplate

- a Higher Power
- the life and words of your inspirational guide
- all that you have to be grateful for
- the wonders of your life
- your unique challenges.

Journal from your heart, considering the life and wisdom of your inspirational guide, and answering some of the questions you selected from this book the night before.

Leave your gift and token in a special place.
You may decide to leave the gift somewhere else, on the way home.
End with a prayer, meditation, or affirmation.
You may wish to use the one at the beginning of this travel template.

THE HOMECOMING

Prepare your homecoming space, prepare your heart, and contemplate these questions:

What did you learn from your personal pilgrimage today?
How will you integrate what you learned into your daily life?
What questions will you live in, during the days ahead?

Journal from your heart.

End with a prayer, meditation, or affirmation.
You may wish to use the one at the beginning of this travel template.

Artist's Cove

Relationships

An interesting way to explore relationships is to discover the relationships artists reveal in their work. The connections that gave artists the images they place before you can tell you something about your own connections. Pay attention to how artists portray shapes and the relationships the shapes have to each other. What subjects do they paint and what does their art reveal about their relationship to those subjects? Art galleries, museums, or exhibits are good places to go in search of art and your own thoughts about relationships.

Prayer, Meditation, or Affirmation for your journey to Artist's Cove:

You can be alone
without being lonely.
You can be in a crowd
without feeling part of it.

UNKNOWN

Date of your personal pilgrimage

HEEDING THE CALL

What called you to this pilgrimage – what questions, what struggles, what events, what people, what challenges?

If you decide to have an inspirational guide on this journey, who will it be?

Why?

Who will bless your journey? (Call him or her before you go.)

THE NIGHT BEFORE

Preparing your space

What ambience do you wish to create and how will you create it? (See page 74 for ideas.)

What rituals or ceremonies might you engage in? (See page 66 for ideas.)

What music will you make or listen to?

Preparing your heart and mind

Start your reading and contemplation with a prayer, meditation, or affirmation. You may wish to use the one at the beginning of this travel template.

Review pages 48 to 51 in this book and select several or all of the questions listed in that section of the book for journaling. The questions are listed below for easy access. Underline the ones you want to contemplate during your journey tomorrow.

1. Which are your primary relationships?
2. How have your relationships changed since you were 8? 18? 28? Today?
3. Where do primary relationships fit among your priorities?
4. Do relationships always take place between and among people? What other things are you in relationship with?
5. How is your relationship with the universe?
6. How is your relationship with yourself?
7. What is the connection between your relationship with the universe and your relationship with yourself?
8. How can you improve some of your work relationships?
9. How can you improve some of your family relationships?
10. What other kinds of relationships do you want to add to your life?

You might also want to answer the following questions: How do the life and wisdom of my inspirational guide speak to these questions?

What do I really want to know?

Travel details

Check list: You have

- ❍ directions to your destination
- ❍ water and snacks
- ❍ your copy of *Personal Pilgrimage at Midlife*
- ❍ a pen or pencil
- ❍ a gift and token to leave behind
- ❍ a blessing from someone
- ❍ an idea of how you will celebrate your homecoming (See page 72 for ideas.)

Saying goodnight

End your evening with a prayer, meditation, or affirmation. You may wish to use the one at the beginning of this travel template.

THE JOURNEY

Begin your day with a prayer, mediation, or affirmation. You may wish to use the one at the beginning of this travel template.

When you arrive at your destination, take time to

- breathe deeply
- pay attention to the details in your surroundings
- touch things around you.

Things you may wish to contemplate

- a Higher Power
- the life and words of your inspirational guide
- all that you have to be grateful for
- the wonders of your life
- your unique challenges.

Journal from your heart, considering the life and wisdom of your inspirational guide, and answering some of the questions you selected from this book the night before.

Leave your gift and token in a special place.
You may decide to leave the gift somewhere else, on the way home.
End with a prayer, meditation, or affirmation.
You may wish to use the one at the beginning of this travel template.

THE HOMECOMING

Prepare your homecoming space, prepare your heart, and contemplate these questions:

What did you learn from your personal pilgrimage today?
How will you integrate what you learned into your daily life?
What questions will you live in, during the days ahead?

Journal from your heart.

End with a prayer, meditation, or affirmation.
You may wish to use the one at the beginning of this travel template.

Quiet Summit

Priorities

Do you know of a place where you can be quiet? Still? At peace? Where a certain hush will allow you to stop and think? Where would that be? The library? The downtown art museum? A particular hilltop? A mountain cabin? This would be a good place for sorting out priorities.

Prayer, Meditation, or Affirmation for your journey to Quiet Summit:

Anything less than a concious commitment to the important
is an unconscious commitment to the unimportant.

STEPHEN COVEY, FIRST THINGS FIRST

Date of your personal pilgrimage

____

HEEDING THE CALL

What called you to this pilgrimage – what questions, what struggles, what events, what people, what challenges?

____

____

____

If you decide to have an inspirational guide on this journey, who will it be?

____

____

____

Why?

Who will bless your journey? (Call him or her before you go.)

THE NIGHT BEFORE

Preparing your space

What ambience do you wish to create and how will you create it? (See page 74 for ideas.)

What rituals or ceremonies might you engage in? (See page 66 for ideas.)

What music will you make or listen to?

Preparing your heart and mind

Start your reading and contemplation with a prayer, meditation, or affirmation. You may wish to use the one at the beginning of this travel template.

Review pages 51 to 55 in this book and select several or all of the questions listed in that section of the book for journaling. The questions are listed below for easy access. Underline the ones you want to contemplate during your journey tomorrow.

1. Have you identified your priorities? If yes, what are the top three? If not, why not?
2. What were your top three priorities when you were 8? 18? 28? How have they changed?
3. How do you know what your priorities are?
4. How often do you evaluate your priorities? Is this often enough?
5. How are your priorities reflected in the way you live your life?
6. Do any of your priorities conflict? If so, how? And how does the conflict affect your peace of mind?
7. Do others understand your priorities?
8. How do your priorities affect your relationships?
9. How do your priorities affect your work?
10. How do your priorities define who you are?

You might also want to answer the following questions: How do the life and wisdom of my inspirational guide speak to these questions?

____

____

____

____

What do I really want to know?

____

____

____

Travel details

Check list: You have

- ❍ directions to your destination
- ❍ water and snacks
- ❍ your copy of *Personal Pilgrimage at Midlife*
- ❍ a pen or pencil
- ❍ a gift and token to leave behind
- ❍ a blessing from someone
- ❍ an idea of how you will celebrate your homecoming (See page 72 for ideas.)

Saying goodnight

End your evening with a prayer, meditation, or affirmation. You may wish to use the one at the beginning of this travel template.

THE JOURNEY

Begin your day with a prayer, mediation, or affirmation. You may wish to use the one at the beginning of this travel template.

Reminder:

Don't forget your pilgrim's satchel with book, pen, directions, water and snacks.

When you arrive at your destination, take time to

- breathe deeply
- pay attention to the details in your surroundings
- touch things around you.

Things you may wish to contemplate

- a Higher Power
- the life and words of your inspirational guide
- all that you have to be grateful for
- the wonders of your life
- your unique challenges.

Journal from your heart, considering the life and wisdom of your inspirational guide, and answering some of the questions you selected from this book the night before.

Mountain connections

Throughout my life, I have been drawn to mountains, but especially in recent years. They beckon me into their rocky folds, calling me to solitary picnics and romantic weekends, for times of contemplation and quiet, for camping with friends and sightseeing with my mom. I love the ride out to our local mountains here in San Diego County, where the slopes are gentle and green. The little mountain town of Julian is a favorite destination for personal pilgrimage among the locals. Perhaps as much for the apple pie as for the natural beauty.

Through recent research and reading, I have come to understand why the mountains seem to beckon me. The ancient Israelites and Hindus believed that the vertical axis of the mountain, drawn from its peak to its base, connected it to the world-axis, which is identified as the center of the world. This powerful symbolism may not be scientifically correct (or perhaps it is, I'm afraid I don't know), but it sounds exactly right to me, and on some level, I believe it is true. And somehow, I believe the powerful center of its geometrical shape makes the mountain – any mountain – an attractor. In other words, I sometimes feel as if huge magnets are housed within the three points of the mountain triangle, and I am being pulled into them. It is as if mountains symbolize my True North, as do the ocean, forests, and other embodiments of nature.

As far as I know, no religion has claimed the local mountains of San Diego, nor Julian, as an official pilgrimage site, though there are certainly sites within these mountains that hosted many a sacred celebration in ancient times. In any event, these mountains frequently call out to me, and I pilgrimage there often – empowered, healed, enlightened, and full of apple pie upon my return.

Leave your gift and token in a special place.
You may decide to leave the gift somewhere else, on the way home.
End with a prayer, meditation, or affirmation.
You may wish to use the one at the beginning of this travel template.

THE HOMECOMING

Prepare your homecoming space, prepare your heart, and contemplate these questions:

What did you learn from your personal pilgrimage today?
How will you integrate what you learned into your daily life?
What questions will you live in, during the days ahead?

Journal from your heart.

End with a prayer, meditation, or affirmation.
You may wish to use the one at the beginning of this travel template.

Stony Place

Loose Ends

Is it time to do a complete inventory of all the things that are yet undone in your life? Relationships without closure, lost things still not found, amends yet to be made, photos to paste, addresses to put in your address book, things you still have to learn how to do? Take an inventory in the presence of a stone or stones that signify solid matter, order, earth anchors. See how everything around you is in order, how everything around you is complete.

Prayer, Meditation, or Affirmation for your journey to Stony Place:

The universe is in order.
My life is in order.

Date of your personal pilgrimage

HEEDING THE CALL

What called you to this pilgrimage – what questions, what struggles, what events, what people, what challenges?

If you decide to have an inspirational guide on this journey, who will it be?

Why?

Who will bless your journey? (Call him or her before you go.)

THE NIGHT BEFORE

Preparing your space

What ambience do you wish to create and how will you create it? (See page 74 for ideas.)

What rituals or ceremonies might you engage in? (See page 66 for ideas.)

What music will you make or listen to?

Preparing your heart and mind

Start your reading and contemplation with a prayer, meditation, or affirmation. You may wish to use the one at the beginning of this travel template.

Review pages 55 to 58 in this book and select several or all of the questions listed in that section of the book for journaling. The questions are listed below for easy access. Underline the ones you want to contemplate during your journey tomorrow.

1. What relationships still need to be mended?
2. What relationships do you need to re-establish?
3. What financial matters still need to be addressed?
4. What family matters are still hanging?
5. Have you lost anything that you have stopped looking for? What is it? Where might it be?
6. What memories do you need to document?
7. What needs to be fixed at your home?
8. What health issues have you been ignoring?
9. What letters do you need to write?
10. What other loose ends do you need to acknowledge?

You might also want to answer the following questions: How do the life and wisdom of my inspirational guide speak to these questions?

What do I really want to know?

Travel details

Check list: You have

- ❍ directions to your destination
- ❍ water and snacks
- ❍ your copy of *Personal Pilgrimage at Midlife*
- ❍ a pen or pencil
- ❍ a gift and token to leave behind
- ❍ a blessing from someone
- ❍ an idea of how you will celebrate your homecoming (See page 72 for ideas.)

Saying goodnight

End your evening with a prayer, meditation, or affirmation. You may wish to use the one at the beginning of this travel template.

THE JOURNEY

Begin your day with a prayer, mediation, or affirmation. You may wish to use the one at the beginning of this travel template.

Reminder:
Don't forget your pilgrim's satchel with book, pen, directions, water and snacks.

When you arrive at your destination, take time to

- breathe deeply
- pay attention to the details in your surroundings
- touch things around you.

Things you may wish to contemplate

- a Higher Power
- the life and words of your inspirational guide
- all that you have to be grateful for
- the wonders of your life
- your unique challenges.

Journal from your heart, considering the life and wisdom of your inspirational guide, and answering some of the questions you selected from this book the night before.

Stone stories

Many cultures have worshipped stones, especially large stones. For instance, though little is known about the purpose or meaning of the megaliths erected across prehistoric Europe, most archaeologists agree that they mark or embellish a sacred place in the landscape.

Small, individual stones have also been imbued with special meaning throughout history. I have a contemporary story of such a stone. A few years ago, while on an Outward Bound adventure in the Puget Sound, I gathered beautiful rocks from the shores of various islands. Sometimes I think it is a miracle that any of them ultimately made it back to San Diego and now adorn the rim around my bathtub, the countertop in my master bath, and the railing around my front deck. The Outward Bound experience was rigorous and memorable, and the stones remind me of all I saw, all I accomplished, and all the wonderful people I met. But mostly the stones remind me of all that I learned about life and about myself.

To me, the stones are all beautiful – gray, black, pink, and cream colors, some multi-colored, some flecked and speckled, some streaked. But one is pure white and appears to glow from within. It is my favorite. I consider it my sacred Puget stone.

The story of my sacred stone and that of yet another, the Stone of Destiny, are not so very different. The story of the Stone of Destiny begins in ancient Judah, where Jacob is said to have used the stone for his pillow. The stone made its way from the Temple of Jerusalem to what is now Ireland, when the daughter of the last king of Judah married into the Irish royal family. Somehow the stone made it to Scotland, and then, after a 13th-century war, King Edward carted it from Edinburgh to Westminster Abbey as a victory relic. In 1996, when royalty from both England and Scotland agreed that the stone rightfully belonged in Scotland, the stone went back to Edinburgh, where it resides today, 700 years after its illustrious British stay.

I don't know how my stones made it to the shores of the Puget Sound, who might have used my sacred stone for a pillow, or what wars my stones have seen; and I don't know where they will be 700 years from now. But they undoubtedly know the deep and personal story of the land, sea, and people connected to them, and they tell an important part of my personal story, as well. For that reason, my sacred stone enjoys a revered place on the altar in my living room, where I am hoping it will stay until some wild adventure, or adventurer, carts it away.

Leave your gift and token in a special place.
You may decide to leave the gift somewhere else, on the way home.
End with a prayer, meditation, or affirmation.
You may wish to use the one at the beginning of this travel template.

THE HOMECOMING

Prepare your homecoming space, prepare your heart, and contemplate these questions:

What did you learn from your personal pilgrimage today?
How will you integrate what you learned into your daily life?
What questions will you live in, during the days ahead?

Journal from your heart.

End with a prayer, meditation, or affirmation.
You may wish to use the one at the beginning of this travel template.

Open Space

Forgiveness

What must you do to forgive? Open your heart. That may not always seem possible. But at this point in your life, it is at least a question to ponder, wondering also, who is left to forgive? Find a place that seems to open into space – where the horizon is the boundary – a field, a rolling lawn, a shoreline, a mountaintop. Feel the openness of the space. Find openness in your heart and mind. Then explore the concept of forgiveness.

Prayer, Meditation, or Affirmation for your journey to Open Space:

To err is human, to forgive divine.

ALEXANDER POPE

Date of your personal pilgrimage

___

HEEDING THE CALL

What called you to this pilgrimage – what questions, what struggles, what events, what people, what challenges?

___

___

___

If you decide to have an inspirational guide on this journey, who will it be?

___

___

___

Why? ___

Who will bless your journey? (Call him or her before you go.)

THE NIGHT BEFORE

Preparing your space

What ambience do you wish to create and how will you create it? (See page 74 for ideas.)

What rituals or ceremonies might you engage in? (See page 66 for ideas.)

What music will you make or listen to?

Preparing your heart and mind

Start your reading and contemplation with a prayer, meditation, or affirmation. You may wish to use the one at the beginning of this travel template.

Review pages 58 to 61 in this book and select several or all of the questions listed in that section of the book for journaling. The questions are listed below for easy access. Underline the ones you want to contemplate during your journey tomorrow.

1. What does it mean to forgive?
2. Who have you forgiven in your life?
3. Who do you need to forgive now?
4. What is difficult about forgiving?
5. Must you forgive?
6. What will happen if you don't forgive?
7. How do you forgive?
8. How does it feel to forgive?
9. Who has forgiven you? How do you know?
10. Do you need to forgive yourself? For what?

You might also want to answer the following questions: How do the life and wisdom of my inspirational guide speak to these questions?

What do I really want to know?

Travel details

Check list: You have

- ❍ directions to your destination
- ❍ water and snacks
- ❍ your copy of *Personal Pilgrimage at Midlife*
- ❍ a pen or pencil
- ❍ a gift and token to leave behind
- ❍ a blessing from someone
- ❍ an idea of how you will celebrate your homecoming (See page 72 for ideas.)

Saying goodnight

End your evening with a prayer, meditation, or affirmation. You may wish to use the one at the beginning of this travel template.

THE JOURNEY

Begin your day with a prayer, mediation, or affirmation. You may wish to use the one at the beginning of this travel template.

Reminder:
Don't forget your pilgrim's satchel with book, pen, directions, water and snacks.

When you arrive at your destination, take time to

- breathe deeply
- pay attention to the details in your surroundings
- touch things around you.

Things you may wish to contemplate

- a Higher Power
- the life and words of your inspirational guide
- all that you have to be grateful for
- the wonders of your life
- your unique challenges.

Journal from your heart, considering the life and wisdom of your inspirational guide, and answering some of the questions you selected from this book the night before.

Leave your gift and token in a special place.
You may decide to leave the gift somewhere else, on the way home.
End with a prayer, meditation, or affirmation.
You may wish to use the one at the beginning of this travel template.

THE HOMECOMING

Prepare your homecoming space, prepare your heart, and contemplate these questions:

What did you learn from your personal pilgrimage today?
How will you integrate what you learned into your daily life?
What questions will you live in, during the days ahead?

Journal from your heart.

End with a prayer, meditation, or affirmation.
You may wish to use the one at the beginning of this travel template.

Familiar Settings

Worldview

This pilgrimage is a bit of a mind-bender and requires a philosophical orientation. Deep thoughts and deep questions!

There's nothing like really seeing a place you thought you'd seen many times before. By going someplace familiar and by examining how it fits into your worldview, or how your perception of the place is affected by your worldview, you will perhaps see things you've not seen before. Worldview is the set of beliefs we hold, often unquestioned and unexamined. It is our assumed reality, the instrument through which we see everything. Try selecting from among the following worldviews: ecological, where everything is connected to everything else; hostile, where we fight continually to survive and sometimes win; friendly, where the world is basically good and in our favor, even when bad things happen; material, where all things outside us are separate from us; spiritual, where the world is powered by a force greater than ourselves. For example, I describe my worldview as ecological, which means that everything is connected to everything else in my world. As I sit at Swami's Beach in Encinitas, I ponder how the ocean is connected to the parking lot, how the parking lot is connected to me, and how we are all connected to my sister, who is sitting at home with her family watching TV. And how is all of that connected to global warming? To the rain forest? To the pyramids? Take yourself somewhere familiar and ask yourself, "How do I view the world I live in? How does that view provide the context for this experience?"

Prayer, Meditation, or Affirmation for your journey to Familiar Settings:

The world is as I see it.

Date of your personal pilgrimage

HEEDING THE CALL

What called you to this pilgrimage – what questions, what struggles, what events, what people, what challenges?

If you decide to have an inspirational guide on this journey, who will it be?

Why?

Who will bless your journey? (Call him or her before you go.)

THE NIGHT BEFORE

Preparing your space

What ambience do you wish to create and how will you create it? (See page 74 for ideas.)

What rituals or ceremonies might you engage in? (See page 66 for ideas.)

What music will you make or listen to? ____________________

____

Preparing your heart and mind

Start your reading and contemplation with a prayer, meditation, or affirmation. You may wish to use the one at the beginning of this travel template.

Review pages 61 to 64 in this book and select several or all of the questions listed in that section of the book for journaling. The questions are listed below for easy access. Underline the ones you want to contemplate during your journey tomorrow.

1. Are we born with evil tendencies? Or do we learn them?
2. How did the earth get here? How did you get here?
3. Is there a Higher Power always present and available to you?
4. Are most people generally cheering for your success, or are they mostly cheering for your demise?
5. Must we compete to survive? Or must we collaborate?
6. What role does humanity play in relation to nature?
7. Why are we here? Why are you here?
8. Does good always triumph over evil? Or is it the other way around?
9. Where did your beliefs about the world come from?
10. How have your beliefs about the world changed since you were 8? 18? 28?

You might also want to answer the following questions: How do the life and wisdom of my inspirational guide speak to these questions?

____

____

____

____

What do I really want to know?

____

____

Travel details

Check list: You have

- ❍ directions to your destination
- ❍ water and snacks
- ❍ your copy of *Personal Pilgrimage at Midlife*
- ❍ a pen or pencil
- ❍ a gift and token to leave behind
- ❍ a blessing from someone
- ❍ an idea of how you will celebrate your homecoming (See page 72 for ideas.)

Saying goodnight

End your evening with a prayer, meditation, or affirmation. You may wish to use the one at the beginning of this travel template.

THE JOURNEY

Begin your day with a prayer, mediation, or affirmation. You may wish to use the one at the beginning of this travel template.

Reminder:

Don't forget your pilgrim's satchel with book, pen, directions, water and snacks.

When you arrive at your destination, take time to

- breathe deeply
- pay attention to the details in your surroundings
- touch things around you.

Things you may wish to contemplate

- a Higher Power
- the life and words of your inspirational guide
- all that you have to be grateful for
- the wonders of your life
- your unique challenges.

Journal from your heart, considering the life and wisdom of your inspirational guide, and answering some of the questions you selected from this book the night before.

Leave your gift and token in a special place.
You may decide to leave the gift somewhere else, on the way home.
End with a prayer, meditation, or affirmation.
You may wish to use the one at the beginning of this travel template.

THE HOMECOMING

Prepare your homecoming space, prepare your heart, and contemplate these questions:

What did you learn from your personal pilgrimage today?
How will you integrate what you learned into your daily life?
What questions will you live in, during the days ahead?

Journal from your heart.

End with a prayer, meditation, or affirmation.
You may wish to use the one at the beginning of this travel template.

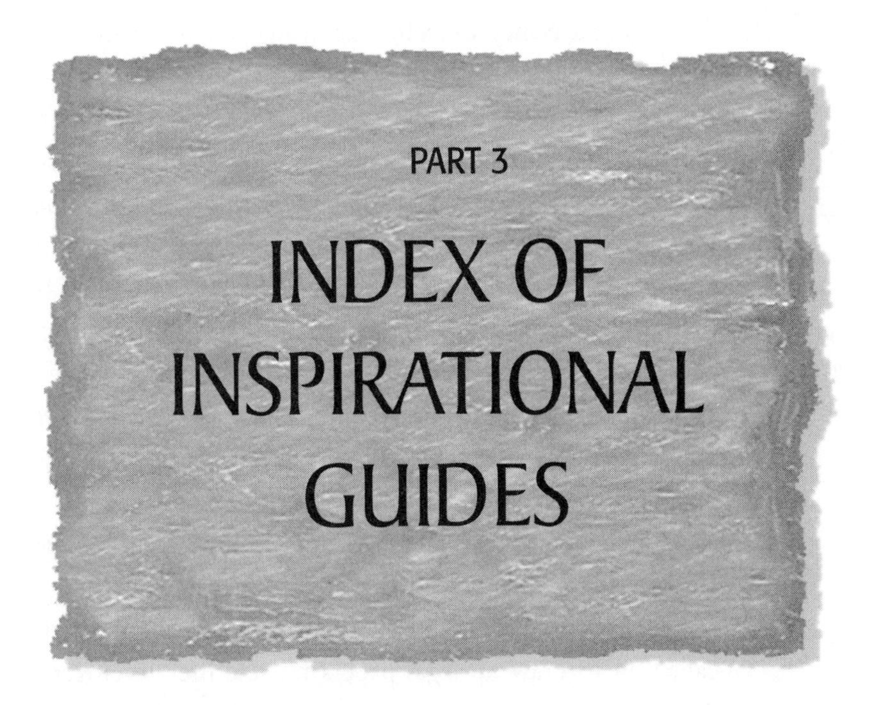

PART 3

INDEX OF INSPIRATIONAL GUIDES

This list of inspirational guides represents some of the people who have inspired me during my own life. It is not perfectly balanced in history, gender, race, or cultural background, but it is relatively diverse and may provide a source of light for you.

Abraham Lincoln

1809–1865

Humble and soft-spoken, yet powerful, U.S. president Abraham Lincoln fought for human rights, exercised a folksy sense of humor, and administered quickly and brilliantly during the gravest of national emergencies.

Abraham Lincoln was the ultimate American success story. Starting out as a backwoods farm boy and rising to the status of one of America's greatest presidents, he became a skilled lawyer, persuasive orator, and administrator of a nation – eloquent and passionate despite his humble ways.

The story of his birth in a log cabin in Kentucky is a true one. Born to Thomas and Nancy Lincoln, Abraham grew to be an industrious boy who worked hard and was especially good with an axe, splitting poles for fence rails. As a presidential candidate, he was known as the Railsplitter.

Abraham also attended school in a log cabin. But he obtained less than one full year of formal education in his entire life. He continued to quest for knowledge, however. At an early age he could read, write, and do simple arithmetic. There were few books besides the family Bible, but he could read that well. He also read classical authors such as Aesop, John Bunyan, and Daniel Defoe, and works such as William Grimshaw's *History of the United States* and Mason Weems' *Life and Memorable Actions of George Washington.* The Washington biography apparently made a lasting impression on Abraham.

Abraham made several moves in his youth – from Kentucky to Indiana to Illinois. He loved to read the newspapers and discuss politics with his friends and neighbors, and because he could read and write, he was often called on to draw up legal papers for less literate citizens. At the age of 23 he decided to run for a seat in the Illinois House of Representatives. He was defeated.

He ran again in 1834, at which time he won and was re-elected for three more two-year terms. He took his first public stand on slavery when the Illinois legislature voted to condemn the activities of the abolition societies. He continued his study of law, married in 1842, and went on to become a master politician in the state of Illinois, as well as a highly respected lawyer. His debates with Senator Douglas are legendary, as the two fought for a Senate seat. The debates brought Abraham national recognition. He was elected to the presidency in 1861 and provided unwavering leadership throughout a war that threatened to rip the country apart. The war began officially in 1861, and throughout, Lincoln took immediate and decisive actions to preserve the Union by defeating the Confederacy.

On November 19, 1863, Lincoln was called upon to deliver a "few appropriate remarks" at a military ceremony honoring the Gettysburg battle. The distinguished orator Edward Everett made the main address, which lasted two hours. Although Abraham's speech was brief, it was a masterpiece in which he rededicated the war effort to the principles of democracy. The Gettysburg Address is considered one of the greatest speeches in history.

Besides the terrible burden of war, Abraham endured many personal trials while in the White House, including the death of his son and the severe mental illness of his wife, Mary. He nevertheless remained devoted to his duties and to preserving the Union.

In 1865, Union victory was proclaimed, and in the same year, Abraham Lincoln was assassinated by a crazed actor named John Wilkes Booth.

Words of Wisdom

Tis better to remain silent and be thought a fool than to speak and remove all doubt.

Nearly all men can stand adversity, so if you want to test a man's character, give him power.

Be sure you put your feet in the right place. Then stand firm.

Barbara McClintock

1902–1992

American genetic scientist and Nobel laureate, Barbara McClintock is most noted for her discovery that genes can transfer their positions on chromosomes, affecting hereditary patterns.

Barbara McClintock was born the third of four children, in Hartford, Connecticut, to an accomplished artist and a physician. She was an outstanding student who loved science from her early school days, settling on genetics as her course of study even before she graduated from college. As a woman, she experienced difficulty receiving recognition in the world of academics. Her outstanding research contributions to the field of genetics went unheralded for many years, until 1983, when she was awarded the Nobel Prize in Physiology or Medicine.

From about the age of three until she began school, Barbara lived in Massachusetts with an aunt and uncle, while Dr. McClintock struggled to establish his medical practice. She returned home to attend school and in 1908 the family moved to Brooklyn, New York. As a youth, she enjoyed her own company and loved to read, but she also liked sports. Both her parents were quite unconventional in their attitudes about child rearing, revering the outside interests of their children, as much as their achievements in school.

Barbara discovered science in high school. She loved to learn and most of all to figure things out. At the time of her graduation, the family situation was difficult. Although Barbara had set her heart on attending Cornell University, the family decided they couldn't afford it. Barbara took a job at an employment agency and spent evenings continuing her education by reading in the library. Days before the semester started, the decision was reversed. Barbara took a train to Ithaca and began her studies at Cornell, where she would earn her doctor of philosophy degree.

Barbara flourished at Cornell both socially and intellectually. She was so well liked that she was elected president of the women's freshman class. Despite her solid social standing, she was more interested in her science studies and decided on genetics as her field even before she had earned her bachelor's degree.

She made a number of groundbreaking discoveries through her work with maize, obtaining her doctorate in botany from Cornell in 1927. Her lengthy research into mobile genetic elements was published in the 1940s and 1950s, but its significance was not appreciated until much later. Her gender, as well as the complexity and uniqueness of her work limited her publishing efforts. Nevertheless, as her theories were tested, it became apparent that she was a groundbreaker. She began to receive awards in the late 1960s, including the Kimber Genetics Award and the National Medal of Science. More accolades came her way sporadically for the next 20 years until finally, in 1983, 35 years after publication of the first evidence supporting her theories that genes move, Barbara was awarded the Nobel Prize. Yet while the money attached to these prizes increased her financial security, she found the ceremonies arduous and the publicity and adulation hard to take. She now longed for her privacy and could not have cared less about the recognition.

She often said she expected to live to 90, and it was so.

Words of Wisdom

When you know you're right, you don't care what others think. You know sooner or later it will come out in the wash.

If you know you are on the right track, if you have this inner knowledge, then nobody can turn you off...no matter what they say.

I know my corn plants intimately and I find it a great pleasure to know them.

Billie Holiday

1915–1959

Lady Day, as Billie Holiday was known, was a jazz and blues singer known for her ability to transform songs into emotional works of art.

Born Eleanora Fagan in Baltimore, Maryland, Billie had an impoverished, rough childhood that was a source of inspiration for her music. The sounds of Louis Armstrong and Bessie Smith, played on a Victrola, supplied her initial motivation for pursuing music as a vocation. She made her singing debut in obscure Harlem nightclubs and went on to become a musical legend, despite her heroin addiction and troubles with the law.

Her father played the guitar for a band and abandoned his wife and children early. Billie was born to a 13-year-old mother who had numerous boyfriends as Billie grew up and who was rarely at home. Her first job was scrubbing floors in a whorehouse. As she found her way to Harlem nightclubs, singing for free, she began to develop her deeply emotional style of delivery. She was discovered by John Hammond one night while performing, and, thanks to him, recorded a few titles with Benny Goodman when she was only 18.

From 1935–1942, she made some of the finest recordings of her career while singing for Count Basie's Orchestra, as well as with the bands of Artie Shaw and Lester Young, combining Louis Armstrong's swing with Bessie Smith's blues sound. Her tours were marred by the racism she had to endure, but she continued to develop her unique style and recorded a number of popular hits. She made history in 1939 with her recording *Strange Fruit*, a strong anti-racism statement that became a permanent part of her repertoire.

Lady Day had no technical voice training, but her inimitable diction, unique phrasing, and dramatic intensity contributed to her special style and grace. Her trademark was a white gardenia, worn in her hair.

Billie's voice was actually at its strongest during her period with Decca Records, from 1944–1949. It was with Decca that she recorded her biggest hit, *Lover Man*. She made one Hollywood movie, in 1946, playing the part of a maid, much to her disgust. However, it was worth it to her to be able to perform on screen with her childhood idol Louis Armstrong.

By the mid-1940s she had become addicted to heroin and spent much of 1947 in jail. The good news was that the notoriety catapulted her to mainstream fame. Her following burgeoned, and she was a sought-after performer.

Billie's final years were riddled with trouble. Although her recordings were popular classics, her voice was deteriorating from heroin use. She had a number of miserable romances and her alcohol consumption was contributing to her physical downturn. She enjoyed one final burst of fame in 1957 when she sang "Fine and Mellow" on *The Sound of Jazz* telecast, but her voice on the 1958 album *Lady in Satin* told the story of her demise. Barely croaking out the words on that album, she continued to convey her sorrows through her voice. She collapsed from a heroin overdose and was arrested while on her deathbed. She died at the age of 44.

Words of Wisdom

Sometimes it's worse to win a fight than to lose.

I'm always making a comeback but nobody ever tells me where I've been.

If I don't have friends, then I ain't got nothin'.

Singing songs like *The Man I Love* or *Porgy* is no more work than sitting down and eating Chinese roast duck, and I love roast duck.

Carl Jung

1875–1961

Swiss psychiatrist Carl Gustav Jung brought mysticism and integration to the practice of psychiatry, establishing the concept of the collective unconscious.

Carl Gustav Jung was born to a Protestant clergyman and his wife, in the small Swiss village of Kessewil. He was a voracious reader throughout his lifetime, a protégé of Freud who broke away and developed his own unique theories about the psyche. He became a prolific writer of scholarly tomes on psychoanalysis.

As a child, he was surrounded by a well-educated extended family. His father started Carl on Latin when he was only six years old, sparking his son's lifelong interest in ancient literature. Besides most modern Western European languages, Carl could read several ancient ones, including Sanskrit, the language of the original Hindu holy books. Though he loved to read and study, he wasn't much of a student in his younger years. Introverted and solitary, he didn't get on with others in school as an adolescent.

Though his first choice for a career was archeology, he went on to study medicine instead, settling eventually on psychiatry as his specialty. In 1903, he married, began teaching classes at the University of Zurich, started his private practice, and invented the concept of word association, in which a patient's responses to stimulus words revealed the patient's psychic state. His work on word association brought him international renown and led him to a close collaboration with Sigmund Freud, whose international reputation as a theorist and psychoanalyst was growing.

The relationship with Freud was invaluable to Carl Jung's own reputation. Freud, in fact, referred to Carl in terms that suggested he would be the heir apparent to the Father of Psychiatry, as Freud was known. With publication of *Psychology and the Unconscious,* however, Jung declared his independence from Freud's narrow sexual interpretation of the libido by showing the parallels between ancient myths and psychotic fantasies, explaining human motivation in terms of a larger creative energy. He resigned as president of the International Psychoanalytic Society and founded what he called the analytical school of psychology.

Carl was especially knowledgeable in the symbolism of complex mystical traditions such as Gnosticism, Alchemy, Kabala, and similar traditions in Hinduism and Buddhism. In addition, he had a capacity for vivid dreaming and occasional visions. In the fall of 1913, he had a vision of a "monstrous" flood engulfing most of Europe and turning to blood. He thought he was becoming psychotic, but in August of that year, World War I broke out and

Carl explained his dreams and visions as a connection between his individual psyche and humanity in general. He went on to formulate theories that made a distinction between the personal unconscious, or the repressed feelings and thoughts developed during an individual's life, and the collective unconscious, or those inherited feelings, thoughts, and memories shared by all humanity.

World War I was a painful period of self-examination for Carl, who delved deeply into his own psyche, flirting with psychosis and fighting to maintain his sanity. After the war, he traveled widely, visiting tribal people in Africa, America, and India. He retired in 1946 and began to retreat from public attention after the death of his wife in 1955. He died in Zurich.

Words of Wisdom

We cannot change anything until we accept it. Condemnation does not liberate, it oppresses.

Neurosis is the suffering of a soul which has not discovered its meaning.

Your vision will become clear only when you look into your heart. Who looks outside, dreams. Who looks inside, awakens.

Carl Sandburg

1878–1967

Carl Sandburg started out as a hobo and became a Pulitzer Prize winner, expressing the American spirit in his prose, biographies, and children's stories.

Born of hard-working Swedish immigrants in a three-room cottage in Galesburg, Illinois, Carl Sandburg was the second of seven children and worked from the time he was a young boy. Whether he was delivering milk, harvesting ice, laying bricks, threshing wheat, or shining shoes, he was part of the working class he wrote of, well able to give it voice.

Before signing on for the Spanish American War in 1898, he spent some time as a hobo, riding the rails, learning and performing folk songs, cooking over open fires. His time in the volunteer army was uneventful. After the war, he attended college for a brief time, leaving without a degree. While in school, Carl met professor Philip Green Wright, a talented scholar and political liberal who encouraged the talented young poet. Carl honed his writing skills and printed his first volume of poetry, *In Reckless Ecstasy,* on his mentor's basement press.

After leaving school, he became politically active in the Wisconsin Social Democratic Party, writing and distributing political pamphlets and literature. He met his wife, Lilian Steichen, at party headquarters in Milwaukee. They were married in 1908. With the responsibilities of marriage and family, he moved back to Chicago and took on work as a reporter at the *Chicago Daily News*, where he wrote feature stories and covered the paper's labor beat.

In 1914, his poem "Chicago" was published in the magazine *Poetry* and he was awarded the magazine's Levinson Prize that same year. His first full-sized volume, *Chicago Poems*, published in 1916, established him as the poet laureate of that industrial city. This poetry established him as Walt Whitman's successor as the proclaimer of the American spirit. His famous "Chicago" poem addressed and described the city and its lines are often learned in high school and college literature classes: "Hog Butcher for the World, /Tool Maker, Stacker of Wheat,/ Player with Railroads and the Nation's Freight Handler;/Stormy, husky, brawling,/City of the Big Shoulders…"

After writing *Rootabaga Stories*, a children's book, Carl's publisher suggested a children's biography on Abraham Lincoln. Instead of a book for children, he wrote a two-volume work on the former president, for adults. This book, *Abraham Lincoln: The Prairie Years*, was his first financial success and a preview of four additional volumes on Lincoln, for which he won the Pulitzer Prize.

Carl Sandburg also became known as a performer of folk songs, which he sang in a craggy voice to simple guitar accompaniment. He collected old songs and related materials in two songbooks. He was a prolific storyteller, as well.

Through the 1940s he continued to write and also to raise a herd of prize-winning goats. He moved to Flat Rock, North Carolina – goats, books, and all – in 1945. He won a second Pulitzer Prize in 1951 for his book *Complete Poems*.

He died at his North Carolina home in 1967, but his ashes were returned to his Galesburg birthplace and placed beneath a red granite boulder there.

Words of Wisdom

Life is like an onion. You peel it off one layer at a time, and sometimes you weep.

A baby is God's opinion that life should go on.

I'm an idealist. I don't know where I'm going, but I'm on my way.

Cesar Chavez

1927–1993

Cesar Chavez worked ceaselessly to liberate his people from injustice.

Cesar Chavez spent most of his life helping to improve the quality of life for migrant farm workers. A soft-spoken, nonviolent activist, he founded the United Farm Workers, led successful boycotts and strikes, fasted, and spoke out fervently for the rights and dignity of poor field workers.

Cesar was born in 1927, in Yuma, Arizona, and learned about injustice early in life, when his father was cheated out of a piece of land he had rightfully earned. Working in the fields from an early age, Cesar also learned firsthand about the intolerable working conditions imposed on migrant workers. Though he bypassed a high school education to help support his family, education became Cesar's passion later in life, as he applied the philosophy, theology, economics, and political science he gleaned from his own reading to the monumental social problems facing him and his fellow laborers.

After serving in the U.S. Navy for four years, Cesar married and subsequently had eight children. At this point, he was especially inspired by the lives of Gandhi and St. Francis, and also by two men who eventually influenced the course of his life: Father Donald McDonnell, who spent many hours discussing labor issues and justice for laborers with Cesar; and Fred Ross, founder of the Community Service Organization, who enlisted him to organize and register voters. From 1952 to 1962, Cesar worked for the CSO, a community action program that focused on self-help for farm workers.

In 1962, Cesar formed the National Farm Workers Association, which was chartered in 1966 by the American Federation of Labor and Congress of Industrial Organizations. The organization was dedicated to organizing farm workers to defend their rights, improve their working conditions, and preserve their dignity. While it took several years for the UFW to take hold, by 1970 the organization had forced grape growers to accept union contracts and had effectively organized most of that industry, at one point claiming 50,000 dues-paying members. Eventually, the migrant worker's cause came to be known as La Causa and was supported by organized labor, religious groups, minorities, and students. Cesar had the foresight to train his union workers and then to send many of them into the cities where they were to use the boycott and the picket as their weapons, always avoiding violence.

Cesar fasted many times to win justice for migrants. In 1968, he went on a well-known water-only, 25-day fast, repeating it in 1972 for 24 days, and again in 1988, this time for 36 days. He completed his 36-day Fast for Life on August 21, 1988, when Reverend Jesse Jackson took up the fast for three days before passing it on to other celebrities and leaders. The fast was passed to Martin Sheen, actor; Edward Olmos, actor; Emilio Estevez, actor; Kerry Kennedy, daughter of Robert Kennedy; Peter Chacon, legislator; Julie Carmen, actress; Danny Glover, actor; Carly Simon, singer; and Whoopi Goldberg, comedienne.

After a particularly hard day on the witness stand in Arizona, helping UFW attorneys defend the union against a lawsuit brought by a giant Salinas, California-based lettuce and vegetable producer, Cesar passed away peacefully in his sleep, in a town about 20 miles from Yuma. Friends found him in bed, a book on Native American crafts in his hand, and a peaceful smile on his face.

Words of Wisdom

The love for justice within us is not only the best part of our being, but also the most true to our nature.

¡Si se puede! (Yes we can!)

It is my deepest belief that only by giving our lives do we find life.

We must understand that the highest form of freedom carries with it the greatest measure of discipline.

Chief Sitting Bull

1831–1890

Considered one of the greatest of all Sioux leaders, Chief Sitting Bull fought ferociously to protect his land and his tribe.

Sitting Bull was born into the Hunkpapa Lakota tribe at Grand River, South Dakota, in 1831. His Sioux name was Tatanka Iyotake and from an early age he was admired for his courage, wisdom, and generosity. His nickname was Hunkesi, meaning "slow," because he never hurried and he did everything with care. He joined his first war party at the age of 14.

From 1863 to1868 he led his people in the fight against U.S. encroachment onto Sioux territory. In 1867, he became the first principal chief of the entire Sioux nation. Shortly thereafter, peace was made with the U.S. government, though Sitting Bull refused to trust the government and failed to attend the peace conference or sign the treaty that promised that the Black Hills would remain in Sioux possession forever.

Sitting Bull's lack of trust was well founded. When gold was discovered in the Black Hills, more than 1000 prospectors camped in the hills and the U.S. government ordered the Sioux to their reservations. Anyone who did not comply with the order was considered hostile and was subject to arrest. Several battles ensued, including the famous Battle of Little Bighorn, where General Custer and his army of more than 250 soldiers died at the hands of the Sioux. Prior to the battle, Chief Sitting Bull participated in the Sun Dance ceremony, where in a trancelike state he received a vision of soldiers falling from the sky. His prediction that all the U.S. soldiers would die at Little Bighorn was accurate.

After his victory at Little Bighorn, Sitting Bull and his followers fled to Canada. A devastating winter, lack of food, and the promise of amnesty brought the Sioux to surrender. Sitting Bull was held prisoner for two years before he was moved to Standing Rock Reservation. In 1885, U.S. officials released him and he joined the Buffalo Bill Wild West Show, touring throughout Europe. Because Sitting Bull remained hostile to settlers, there is speculation that permission to travel with the wild west troupe was given to keep the chief from creating problems. He returned to the reservation in 1889.

Sitting Bull remained a powerful force among his people and upon his return to the U.S. would counsel the tribal chiefs, who greatly valued his wisdom. Shortly after his return, the federal government again wanted to break up the tribal lands. They persuaded several government-appointed chiefs to sign an agreement whereby the reservation was divided up and subsequently distributed among the tribal members. Missing from the list of recipients was Sitting Bull's name. Jealousy and fighting broke out among the Lakota, which ultimately contributed to the chief's death.

In addition, the U.S. government wanted to stop a budding new Native religion called the Ghost Dance, which asserted that an Indian messiah would return their lands. As a precaution, tribal police attempted to arrest Sitting Bull. He was killed as his warriors attempted to rescue him.

Words of Wisdom

The earth has received the embrace of the sun and we shall see the results of that love.

Each man is good in the sight of the Great Spirit.

If a man loses anything and goes back and looks carefully for it, he will find it.

Eleanor Roosevelt

1884–1962

Eleanor Roosevelt was a social activist, lecturer, U.S. representative to the United Nations, author, and the wife of U.S. President Franklin D. Roosevelt.

Born in New York City, Eleanor Roosevelt was the daughter of Anna and Elliott Roosevelt, who was President Teddy Roosevelt's younger brother. Her mother died when she was eight and her father when she was ten. Her grandmother sent her to boarding school in England, where she learned a few social graces. Upon her return she was introduced at her debut, where she met distant cousin Franklin Roosevelt. She enrolled in the Junior League of New York, where she taught calisthenics and dancing to immigrants. She also joined the Consumers League and investigated working conditions in the garment districts. In 1905, she married her cousin and within five years they had four children, though one died in early childhood from influenza.

By 1916 Eleanor and Franklin had had six children. In 1918, while assisting with his mail, Eleanor discovered letters revealing his affair with her personal secretary. She offered him a divorce, but he realized the effects on their children, his mistress, and his political future, so he initiated a reconciliation. While Eleanor continued to help her husband politically, she distanced herself from him and his family, and began her own agenda. This was the beginning of her devotion to causes benefiting victims of poverty, prejudice, and war.

When she became First Lady in 1933, Eleanor Roosevelt well understood the social conditions and needs of her country. She became the first president's wife to hold all-female press conferences, on her own. She gave lectures and radio broadcasts, and she even wrote a syndicated newspaper column. During the years that followed, she assisted with the formation of the national Youth Administration and she coordinated meetings between FDR and the NAACP. In 1936, Eleanor gave an impromptu speech at the Democratic National Convention, which helped FDR win an unprecedented third term in office. In 1943 she toured the South Pacific to boost soldier morale. Her husband died two years later.

Americans came to know the Roosevelt home in New York City well. It served as the summer White House and many international dignitaries were entertained there. In 1939, Franklin deeded Hyde Park to the nation as a National Historic Site. In 1940, the Franklin D. Roosevelt Library adjacent to the house was dedicated.

In 1946, Eleanor was elected as head of the United Nations Human Rights Commission, drafting the Declaration of Human Rights. She resigned her U.N. position when Eisenhower became president and traveled the world giving speeches on behalf of the American Association for the United Nations. As late as 1961, when President Kennedy re-appointed her to the United Nations, she spearheaded an ad hoc Commission of Inquiry into the administration of justice in the freedom struggle and she monitored the progress of the fight for civil rights in the United States. She died of tuberculosis at the age of 88 and is buried next to her husband at Hyde Park.

Words of Wisdom

No one can make you feel inferior without your consent.

I think, somehow, we learn who we really are and then live with that decision.

As for accomplishment, I just did what I had to do as things came along.

Elizabeth Blackwell

1821–1910

Elizabeth Blackwell was the first woman doctor in the United States.

Not only was Elizabeth Blackwell the first woman to receive a medical degree in the United States, she opened an infirmary for women and children in New York, confronted prejudice, and authored outstanding health books. She set up a medical college for women and formed a National Health Society in England. In addition, she was active in the women's rights movement from its earliest days.

The Blackwells moved from England, where Elizabeth was born, to New York City in 1832, when Samuel Blackwell's sugar refinery was consumed in a fire. Although Elizabeth's father opened another refinery in the United States, his idealistic attempts to use beet sugar rather than cane sugar (which was produced by slave labor) were unsuccessful. He was a social activist who believed in women's rights, temperance, and the elimination of slavery. The liberal beliefs in the Blackwell household had a profound effect on Elizabeth.

After her father died in 1838, Elizabeth took a teaching job and taught until 1847, when she was finally admitted to medical school. She was initially turned down by every school she applied to, but was finally accepted at Geneva College in New York. Her admittance was initially a joke. The administration was hesitant to admit a woman and threw the decision to the students, who laughingly voted yes. When she arrived, Elizabeth encountered hostility, but she persevered and graduated first in her class in 1849.

After a brief stint of studying in Europe, she returned to New York, where she wanted to open her practice. Because she was a woman, she was unable to work in city dispensaries and hospitals and was unable to rent appropriate quarters for her practice. In 1853, she opened a clinic in a poor section of the city, where she treated women and children. The clinic gradually expanded into a hospital – the New York Infirmary for Women and Children.

After the outbreak of the Civil War, Elizabeth helped form the Woman's Central Relief Association in New York City, which was instrumental in establishing the United States Sanitary Commission, a large organization that aided the Union army by providing food, clothing, medical supplies, and services to soldiers. Once the Civil War was over, Elizabeth began to work toward her long-held dream of setting up a medical college for women. This dream was realized in 1868 with the opening of the Women's Medical College of the New York Infirmary, in New York City.

During the next 30 years, she published numerous books and pamphlets about medicine and education, stating her belief that disease could be prevented by proper hygiene and public sanitation. She also wrote that medical ills were often caused by problems in society, such as poverty and lack of education. She was involved in women's rights activities and was included in the *Fortnightly Journal*'s list of 600 prominent women for suffrage. She died in Hastings, England, at the age of 89.

Words of Wisdom

Perseverance and discipline are keys that open many doors.

It is not easy to be a pioneer – but oh, it is fascinating! I would not trade one moment, even the worst moment, for all the riches in the world.

It is well worth a lifetime to have attained knowledge which justifies an attack on the root of all evil – which asserts that because forms of evil have always existed in society, therefore they must always exist.

Emily Dickinson

1830–1886

One of America's best-loved and well-known female poets, Emily Dickinson tackled a myriad of profound subjects, such as the terrors of war, God and religion, the importance of humor, love and sexuality, and death.

Emily Dickinson is thought of as the model of unrequited love, a lifelong spinster who dressed in all-white, a recluse who found refuge in her poetry. In truth, she enjoyed intense and rewarding relationships throughout her life, despite her unmarried state, and ultimately had a profound effect on literature and the poetic genre, despite the fact that only about ten of her nearly 2,000 poems were ever published during her lifetime.

She was the middle child of a prominent Massachusetts family, attending school in Amherst and living in the same house from 1855 until her death in 1886. She, her older brother Austin, and her younger sister Lavinia, lived a quiet, reserved family life, where her father, a well-respected lawyer, exerted absolute authority, and her mother was generally cool and unavailable to provide support and nurturing. The family was rooted in the puritanical Massachusetts of the early 19th century, so the children were naturally raised in the Christian tradition. Though Emily's earliest literary influence was the Holy Bible, she later challenged her family's religious viewpoint and wrote of her own spiritual perspective with little reservation.

Emily has been described as delicate of feature and quiet in nature – pale skin, soft auburn hair, and a small voice. Whether she was a recluse or not is a matter of some debate. Although she seldom left her home, Emily maintained significant relationships with a number of people. Thomas Wentworth Higginson, for instance, was a literary expert who admired her creativity and became her writing mentor, though he suggested that she not pursue publication of her work. In addition, she was her younger sister's faithful lifetime companion, though neither ever married. Emily also maintained lengthy correspondence with a number of people, including her sister-in-law Susan Dickinson, even though they were next-door neighbors. She also wrote to school friends, her cousins, and several patrons of the arts. In fact, some accounts of Emily describe her as an accomplished hostess who entertained guests at her home and at the home of her brother and sister-in-law during her 20s and 30s. One friend commented that Emily was so surrounded by friends at a party, there was no chance to talk with her.

The mystery surrounding Emily's life came from rumors about her unrequited love for a married pastor, Charles Wadsworth. Since many of her poems spoke of passionate love and even alluded to sex, many believed that much of her poetry was an expression of her love for Charles. It is believed that Dickinson's first editors described her and her work to conform to 19th-century stereotypes of women writers, which accounts for her depiction as an isolated, lonely, pining woman. Who she really was may lie somewhere between rumor and misunderstanding.

As a result of Emily's secluded life, she may have been able to focus on her world more closely than her contemporaries could. She drew mostly on the Bible, classical mythology, and Shakespeare for allusions and references. She wrote many of her poems on scraps of paper and left them around the house. Her editors later arranged and classified her work.

Words of Wisdom

To live is so startling it leaves little time for anything else.

Because I could not stop for Death,
He kindly stopped for me.

The soul should always stand ajar. Ready to welcome the ecstatic experience.

Some keep the Sabbath going to Church.

Indira Gandhi

1917–1984

Controversial, brilliant and fiercely determined, Indira Gandhi was the first woman ever elected to lead a democracy.

Indira Gandhi braved political battles all her life, starting at the age of 12 when she served as spokesperson for the Monkey Brigade, a youth group dedicated to ending British rule of India. Her assassination ended a brilliant but stormy political career.

Indira was the only child of Jawaharlal and Kamala Nehru and therefore grew up in a highly political household. Her father was a lawyer, a nationalist leader, and the first prime minister of India from 1947 to 1964. Her mother died when Indira was 19.

After her brief first forays into the public arena via the Monkey Brigade, Indira began her college studies at Visva-Bharti University in Bengal and went on to the University of Oxford in England. She had always longed to join the Indian National Congress, the political organization spearheading the fight for Indian independence from British rule, and she did so at the age of 21. Three years later she was married to a lawyer also active in the Congress. Shortly after their marriage, the two were imprisoned for about eight months on the charge of civil disobedience.

The year that India won its independence – 1947 – Indira's father was elected prime minister. She moved into his home with her family and traveled as his hostess and confidant, meeting famous political figures and gaining valuable experience. She was elected to the National Congress Party's executive branch in 1955 and became the party's president in 1959. When her father died in 1964, she was appointed minister of information and broadcasting, which was the fourth highest ranking position in the cabinet. Many Indians were illiterate, so radio and television played a major role in informing the public. As minister, Indira encouraged production of inexpensive radios and television sets. When her father's successor died in 1966, she was eventually elected the new prime minister, making her the first woman ever elected to lead a democracy.

Indira Gandhi's main accomplishments were improving relations with the Soviet Union and victory in the 1971 war with Pakistan. Also in 1971, under Indira Gandhi's administration, India sent its first satellite into space. India enjoyed one of the fastest growing economies in the world toward the end of her time as prime minister.

Indira used her international savvy to build alliances, including a relationship with the United States, which ultimately provided her country with assistance on several occasions. Within her own government she enjoyed times of prosperity and popularity, as well as severe criticism for some of her harsher, more controlling moves to squelch opposition. In her later years, Indira didn't seem to trust her own political advisers or allies, except for members of her own family. She groomed both her sons to follow her in her political pursuits.

Two of Indira's bodyguards assassinated her in reaction to her aggressive attempts to eliminate terrorists. Her son Rajiv was sworn in as prime minister within 24 hours of her death. He led his party to a resounding victory – the greatest election victory for the Congress Party since India's independence, which he attributed to his mother's martyrdom.

Words of Wisdom

You must learn to be still in the midst of activity and to be vibrantly alive in repose.

My grandfather once told me that there were two kinds of people: those who do the work and those who take the credit. He told me to try to be in the first group; there was much less competition.

You cannot shake hands with a clenched fist.

Martyrdom does not end something, it is only a beginning.

Lucille Ball

1911–1989

Lucille Ball was a highly successful comedienne and talented actress famous for portraying the character Lucy Ricardo in the classic *I Love Lucy* television series.

Lucille Ball left home for acting school at the age of 15. Though her acting teachers told her she was wasting her time, she wound up with acting credits on a total of 73 movies, a starring role in America's most popular TV series, ownership of a highly successful television production company, and four Emmy Awards for her comedic and acting talents.

Because acting didn't appear to be her strength in the beginning, Lucy took a job as a model in New York, using the name Diane Belmont. She was moderately successful, winning national exposure as the Chesterfield Cigarette Girl in the early 1930s. She continued to take minor acting roles. By the late 1940s, she had appeared in more than 60 movies, including feature films starring Katharine Hepburn, Ginger Rogers, and Bob Hope.

After performing in the musical *Too Many Girls* in 1940 with popular Cuban band leader Desi Arnaz, Ball fell in love with her co-star and married him later that year. Band and career schedules clashed often and the newlyweds frequently found themselves on opposite sides of the country. Lucy filed for divorce in 1944, but the two managed to patch things up just one day before the divorce was to be finalized.

In an effort to save the marriage, the two decided to conceive a television series together. They pitched the idea to CBS, who balked at the idea at first, claiming that the theme of the series – ditzy redhead marries Latin band leader and proceeds to drive everyone crazy with her desire to be in pictures – would never go over. So Desi and Lucy formed their own production company and eventually brought *I Love Lucy* to the airwaves in 1951. It instantly became America's most popular TV show. During its first four years on the air, the show was number one in the Nielsen ratings. During its entire history, the show never fell below number three. *I Love Lucy* won more than 200 awards, five Emmys, and the love of a nation.

Various versions of *I Love Lucy* followed the original show when it left the air in 1957, all relatively successful. Lucy and Desi divorced in 1960. She married nightclub comedian Gary Morton and bought Desi's interest in Desilu Productions, eventually selling it for a net profit of $10 million. Desilu produced some of the most successful series in television history, including *The Untouchables*, *Star Trek*, and *Mission Impossible*.

At the age of 62, Lucy went outside the boundaries of comedy and won wide acclaim for her appearance on Broadway's *Wildcat*. She also co-starred with Bob Hope in two feature films and with Henry Fonda in the critically acclaimed *Yours, Mine and Ours*. At 74, she played the part of a homeless woman in the TV film *Stone Pillow*. Her last public appearance was at the 1989 Academy Awards.

Words of Wisdom

One of the things I learned the hard way was that it doesn't pay to get discouraged. Keeping busy and making optimism a way of life can restore your faith in yourself.

I don't know anything about luck. I've never banked on it and I'm afraid of people who do. Luck to me is something else: hard work – and realizing what is opportunity and what isn't.

I think knowing what you cannot do is as important as knowing what you can do. In fact, that's good taste.

Martha Graham

1893–1991

Martha Graham was an influential American modern dancer, choreographer, and teacher.

Martha Graham started her dancing career at the relatively late age of 22. She performed her first solo recital at the age of 33, after 10 years as a student and teacher at various dance studios. By 1930 she was working steadily with her own company, the Dance Repertory Theater, creating a controversial, unique style of performance, both hailed and criticized by critics worldwide throughout her lifetime.

Because her father was a puritanical Scottish doctor, Martha wasn't allowed to pursue the art of dance until he died. After seeing a performance in Los Angeles, she knew her passion was dancing and pursued it with a vengeance. In her early work, she rejected the ornate style of her day in favor of more sparse staging. Her austere staging and costumes, as well as the sharp movements of her choreography, were bewildering for audiences initially, but they warmed to her creativity as her highly individual and expressive style developed.

She trained young dancers for her company, developing a technique – the most consistent and thorough in American modern dance – that included the contraction and release of different parts of the body; close relation of breathing to feeling and movement; austere, angular body lines; and close contact with the ground. The flexed foot and pulsating pelvis became a Graham trademark, the emotional building blocks of modern dance.

She made full and often symbolic use of the traditional resources of the theater, including lighting, stage sets and properties, and costuming. Her stage settings, which were often abstract and sculptural, were executed by notable artists, particularly the American sculptor Isamu Noguchi. As her fame grew and the Martha Graham School of Dance began to attract talented young dancers, Martha gathered famed composers to illustrate her epic ballets, many of which addressed achievements of historical women, from Emily Dickinson to Joan of Arc. After 1934, she used only music composed specifically for her dances by such composers as Aaron Copland, who wrote his classic *Appalachian Spring* for her. She choreographed for it an interpretation of a Quaker wedding that remains her best remembered work.

Martha's work varies in mood from the witty *Every Soul Is a Circus* to the frenzied *Deaths and Entrances*, which was based on the Brontë family, with Emily as the heroine. In 1984, at the age of 90, she choreographed *The Rite of Spring* by Russian American composer Igor Stravinsky.

Martha created more than 150 works in 50 years, with the height of her career in the 1940s. She produced 52 shows with Jean Rosenthal over a span of 37 years. She was the first dancer to receive a Guggenheim Foundation Fellowship, and she was honored with the Medal of Freedom at the end of her career.

She worked almost to the end of her long life. She died at the age of 97 in New York City.

Words of Wisdom

The past is not dead; it is not even past. People live on inner time.

There is a vitality, a life force, an energy, a quickening that is translated through you into action, and because there is only one of you in all of time, this expression is unique. And if you block it, it will never exist through any other medium. The world will not have it. It isn't your business to determine how good it is, nor how it compares with other expressions. It is your business to keep it yours clearly and directly; to keep the channel open.

Life today is nervous, sharp, and zig-zag. It often stops in mid air...It is what I want for my dances.

Martin Luther King, Jr.

1929–1968

An eloquent Baptist minister, Martin Luther King, Jr. led the civil rights movement in America until his death by assassination in 1968. He was awarded the Nobel Peace Prize for his efforts to achieve civil rights reform through nonviolent means.

Martin Luther King, Jr. was born in Atlanta, Georgia, and rose to prominence during the civil rights movement through his activism, eloquence, and determination. Adopting the nonviolent methods of protest used by Mohandas Gandhi in India, he steadfastly maintained that victory for blacks could not come from the same violent means used against them. His concerns broadened from civil rights to include the violence of the Vietnam War and the violence of poverty. He won the Nobel Peace Prize in 1964.

Martin came from a line of Baptist ministers. His grandfather was one, and his father, as well. He earned a bachelor of divinity degree in 1955, acquainting himself with the teachings of Gandhi. Soon thereafter he was asked to lead a bus boycott in Montgomery, Alabama. The city's black leaders had organized the boycott to protest enforced racial segregation in public transportation after the arrest of Rosa Parks, an African-American woman who had refused to give up her seat to a white passenger. In the course of the 381-day boycott, King was arrested and jailed, his home was bombed, and many threats were made against his life. The boycott ended in 1956 with a mandate from the Supreme Court outlawing all segregated public transportation in the city. The boycott was a victory for nonviolent protest and King emerged a highly respected leader.

Martin went to India to meet Gandhi's followers in 1959, so that he could more clearly work out his understanding of the Great One's principle of nonviolent persuasion. Shortly thereafter he gave up his pastorate in Montgomery to co-pastor, with his father, Ebenezer Baptist Church in Atlanta, a strategic move that enabled him to participate more effectively in the national leadership of the burgeoning civil rights movement. Though his nonviolent methods were not universally popular among blacks, some of whom were impatient and angry, his prestige ensured that nonviolence remained the official mode of resistance. In 1963, he led a massive civil rights campaign in Birmingham, Alabama, and organized drives for black voter registration, desegregation, and better education and housing throughout the South. During these nonviolent campaigns, he was arrested several times. In 1963, he led the historic March on Washington, where he delivered his famous "I Have a Dream" speech.

By the mid-1960s, Martin's concerns had broadened to include the Vietnam War. His association with the antiwar movement and its national white leadership was controversial to many blacks and Martin began to suffer from exhaustion from stress. His speeches continually alluded to his imminent death. In 1968, he died at the hands of James Earl Ray, who was arrested for murder. More than 100,000 people attended Martin's funeral in Atlanta. In 1983, the third Monday in January was designated a federal legal holiday in honor of Martin Luther King, Jr.'s birthday. His Atlanta birthplace and gravesite were made national historic sites.

Words of Wisdom

Darkness cannot drive out darkness; only light can do that.

If a man hasn't discovered something that he will die for, he isn't fit to live.

I have a dream.

Mary Baker Eddy

1821–1910

As founder of Christian Science, Mary Baker Eddy was recognized by the National Women's Hall of Fame as the only woman in history to found a major world religion.

Mary Baker Eddy spent much of her life as an invalid, until her encounter at the age of about 40 with Dr. Phineas Quimby. Quimby's method of healing did not include drugs such as the chloroform, vapors, camphor, and ether of her time. After Dr. Quimby died, Mary went on to craft her own philosophy about health and healing, based largely on scripture from the Holy Bible, the idea that illness is fear-based and that divine healing is within. Eventually she founded the Church of Christ, Scientist and the revered *Christian Science Monitor* newspaper.

Mary Baker Eddy had always hungered for truth. Raised with Puritan values and daily Bible reading, as well as talk of God's healing power, she spent many years searching for cures for her physical maladies with available methods. While she sought spiritual guidance, she never found the healing she so desperately needed until she met up with Dr. Quimby.

Dr. Quimby's approach to medicine was curious at the time, as it included no pharmaceuticals. He spoke to her of the role of fear in illness, and of how to combat it. Mental exercises played a major role in eradicating illness and encouraging health, according to Dr. Quimby, and Mary Baker Eddy embraced his philosophy. Upon his death in 1866, she fell on the ice and injured her back, fearing she would never recover. However, after reading an account of one of Jesus' healings in the New Testament, she was instantly cured and truly understood the power of faith in the healing process. She began to formulate her philosophy into what she called *Christian Science.*

She was a lonely figure in the first years of her teaching Christian Science, finding a student here and there, and lecturing to small classes. In addition, there was some controversy about whether her philosophy was her own, or whether she had stolen it from Dr. Quimby. Several court cases established her ownership of the Christian Science tenets expounded in her teachings.

In 1875, she published *Science and Health with Key to the Scriptures,* which was the first Christian Science textbook. She formally founded the Church of Christ, Scientist in 1879. The book is published in 17 languages and Braille, and in audio cassette, CD and electronic form. Over nine million copies have been sold to date and it remains a bestseller each year. She also wrote and published several other books on Christian Science, which have been translated into foreign languages. By the time she died in 1910, the Church of Christ, Scientist, had spread throughout much of the world. One of her greatest accomplishments was founding *The Christian Science Monitor,* a newspaper recognized worldwide for its editorial integrity and news insight.

Mary Baker Eddy has been widely recognized for her spiritual leadership. In 1992, the Women's National Book Association named *Science and Health* as one of 75 books by women "whose words have changed the world." In 1995, she was elected to the National Women's Hall of Fame for leaving "an indelible mark on society, religion, and journalism."

Words of Wisdom

The universe is in us.

True prayer is not asking God for love; it is learning to love, and to include all mankind in one affection.

Reject hatred without hating.

Nelson Mandela

1918–

Nelson Mandela spent nearly 30 years in prison before becoming South Africa's first democratically elected president.

Nelson Mandela was groomed for the position of chieftain of the Thembu tribe, after the death of his father, who was chief. Instead, Nelson chose to become a lawyer. An activist from his earliest years, he wound up in prison, with a life sentence, for protesting the severe racial segregation known as apartheid in South Africa. After his release in 1990, he won the Nobel Peace Prize and was elected president of his country.

Hearing his elders' stories of his ancestors' struggle for freedom, the young Nelson Mandela was moved to make an active contribution to that same struggle. After receiving his primary education at a local mission school, he attended a Wesleyan high school and later enrolled in the University College of Fort Hare. He was suspended from college for joining in a protest boycott and went to Johannesburg, where he completed his law degree by correspondence. He entered politics in earnest while studying in Johannesburg, joining the African National Congress in 1942.

In 1944, he helped form the African National Congress Youth League and was elected national volunteer-in-chief of the 1952 Defiance Campaign. He traveled the country organizing resistance to discriminatory legislation. By 1952 he had opened the first black legal firm in the country and for the next ten years continued his fight for equality and freedom. In 1961, he met and married Nomazmo Madikizela (Winnie); the two separated in 1992.

In 1962, he left South Africa for military training in Algeria. Upon his return, he was arrested for leaving the country illegally. While serving his five-year sentence, he was sentenced again, this time for treason, and this time for life.

Robben Island, where he was imprisoned, became a center for learning and Mandela was a central figure in the organized political education classes there. He became a worldwide symbol of resistance to white domination in South Africa. He never compromised his political principles and was always a source of strength for the other prisoners, refusing twice the offer of release in exchange for compromising his passionate political viewpoints. Prisoners, he said, cannot enter into legal contracts, only free men can do so.

He was released in 1990 by President F. W. de Klerk, who also lifted the ban on the African National Congress. Mandela assumed leadership of the ANC and with his delegation agreed to suspend armed struggle. He led negotiations with the government for a new constitution that would grant political power to the country's black majority population. In 1991, the government repealed the last of the laws that formed the legal basis for apartheid. Mandela and de Klerk shared the 1993 Nobel Peace Prize for their effort in establishing democracy and racial harmony in South Africa. Nelson was elected president of South Africa in 1994. He holds honorary degrees from more than 50 international universities and is chancellor of the university of the North.

Words of Wisdom

A good head and a good heart are always a formidable combination.

You can never have an impact on society if you have not changed yourself... Great peacemakers are all people of integrity, of honesty, of humility.

That was one of the things that worried me – to be raised to the position of a semi-god – because then you are no longer a human being. I wanted to be known as Mandela, a man with weaknesses, some of which are fundamental, and a man who is committed, but nevertheless, sometimes he fails to live up to expectations.

Oprah Winfrey

1954–

Influential trend-setter and accomplished media celebrity, Oprah Winfrey has focused the attention of the world on the importance of spirit.

Oprah Winfrey, born in 1954 in Kosciusko, Mississippi, has risen above poverty and abuse in her childhood to enjoy an accomplishment-studded adulthood. From her early career as a news anchor in Nashville, Tennessee, in the early 1970s, to her current, wildly popular *The Oprah Winfrey Show,* she has become a cornerstone to public discourse and stands as a beacon to success.

She was born to unmarried parents and raised by her paternal grandmother. Her earliest years were spent living on a farm. By age three she was reading the Bible and reciting in church.

In 1960, she joined her mother in Milwaukee, where she endured sexual abuse from male relatives. She moved to her father's home when she was 13 and gave birth to a premature baby at the age of 14. Books were her best friends in junior high school, and throughout high school she excelled, eventually winning a full scholarship to Tennessee State University. She was crowned Miss Fire Prevention in Nashville at the age of 17. Her poise in front of audiences, as well as her intelligence, charm, and good looks, helped her win beauty contests, where she received her first public attention.

On a lark, she read news copy at a local Nashville radio station and was promptly hired to read news professionally on the air. In 1973, she became the first African-American and the first woman to anchor a television newscast in Nashville, Tennessee. By 1977, she had shed her role as news anchor and had found her niche as a talk show host on *People Are Talking*, a morning show in Baltimore, Maryland. She then went on to Chicago to host *A.M. Chicago*, where her ratings surpassed Phil Donahue's. In 1986, her show went national and was renamed *The Oprah Winfrey Show*. That same year she was nominated for an Oscar for her role in *The Color Purple*. She formed Harpo Productions the following year, becoming the third woman to own her own major film studio.

Oprah proposed the National Child Protection Act in 1991 and testified before the U.S. Senate Judiciary about her own sexual abuse as a child. The Act was signed into law in 1993.

In 1996, Oprah launched her popular book club; in 1998 she produced and starred in Toni Morrison's *Beloved;* and in 1999 she established *O* magazine. *The Oprah Winfrey Show* has become the highest rated talk show in television history, with 25 Emmy Awards.

Oprah has established the "world's largest piggy bank," where people all over the world contribute spare change to raise money (matched by Oprah) to send disadvantaged kids to college. Her philanthropic efforts are legendary.

In addition, she has focused attention on the soul of America, asking her viewers to honor their spirits in various ways. Featuring the inspirational stories not only of celebrities but of her loyal fans, her television show attracts 14 million viewers daily in the United States and millions more in 132 other countries. She has accumulated a personal fortune estimated at more than half a billion dollars. In 1996, *Time* magazine named her one of the 25 most influential people in the world.

Words of Wisdom

Always continue the climb. It is possible for you to do whatever you choose, if you first get to know who you are and are willing to work with a power that is greater than ourselves to do it.

Think like a queen. A queen is not afraid to fail. Failure is another steppingstone to greatness.

If you want to accomplish the goals of your life, you have to begin with the Spirit.

You can have it all. You just can't have it all at one time.

Paul McCartney

1942–

A gifted songwriter, musician, and member of the Beatles, Paul McCartney helped revolutionize popular music of the 1960s and 1970s.

James Paul McCartney was born into a working-class family in Liverpool, England, and suffered the loss of his mother to breast cancer when he was 14 years old. For consolation, his father Jim bought him a guitar and Paul was forevermore attached to it. His father worked as a salesman for a cotton brokerage firm by day and by night he himself was a musician with the Jim Mac Jazz Band. He was delighted at his son's interest in music.

Paul met John Lennon through a mutual friend, who invited Paul to see John play with The Quarrymen. He was introduced to John, played guitar for him, and was instantly asked to join the band. Paul accepted and the two began collaborating immediately. Paul and John performed together in several groups before forming the Beatles in 1959.

While with the Beatles, Paul played bass and wrote both music and lyrics with John. Together they formed a successful songwriting partnership, combining Paul's wistful lyricism with John's intellectual depth and hard rock sound. Some of their better-known compositions include *Yesterday, Eleanor Rigby, Penny Lane,* and *Let It Be.*

In 1969, Paul broke off a five-year relationship with actress Jane Asher to date American photographer Linda Eastman. He adopted Linda's daughter Heather and the couple went on to have three of their own children – Mary, Stella, and James. With the break-up of the Beatles in 1970, Paul released his first solo album, *McCartney*, which contains the international hit *Maybe I'm Amazed.* Throughout the 1970s, he collaborated with his wife to produce a number of hit albums, touring internationally with his band, Wings. Linda was not only his biggest supporter, she played keyboard and sang back-up in the band. On tour following the release of the 1979 Wings album *Back to the Egg*, Paul was arrested for marijuana possession in Japan and spent a nerve-wracking ten days in jail, denied even the comfort of a pen and paper to record his thoughts. When he was released, thanks to diplomatic efforts, he finally disbanded Wings and released the solo effort *McCartney II.*

In 1995, Linda McCartney was diagnosed with breast cancer and underwent surgery. Two years later, she and Paul announced that she was in remission and on the road to a total recovery. In March of 1998, however, they were shocked to learn that the cancer had spread to her liver. The following month, while the couple was vacationing in California, Linda's condition suddenly worsened, and she died at the age of 56. The McCartneys were so devoted to each other, according to their publicist, that during the course of their almost 30-year marriage, the only time they had spent a night apart was when Paul served his jail sentence in Tokyo.

Paul was formally knighted Sir Paul by Queen Elizabeth in 1997 for his "cultural contributions and service to music." He dedicated his knighthood to fellow ex-Beatles Ringo Starr, George Harrison, and the late John Lennon.

Words of Wisdom

We have learned that change comes slowly.

Music is such a beautiful innocent thing for me, a *magic* thing.

I love a choir.

Pierre Elliott Trudeau

1919–1999

Pierre Trudeau was a flamboyant and articulate intellectual who rose to become one of Canada's greatest prime ministers.

Pierre's father was a wealthy Quebecois; his mother was of Scottish descent. His given name, Pierre Elliott, thus represented the bilingual, bicultural personality of Canada and the federalism he fought so hard to preserve. The Trudeau family often went on extensive European tours, allowing Pierre to become a world traveler at a young age.

He studied at Jean de Brebeuf College, a Jesuit institution where he probably acquired his lifelong motto of "reason over passion." He earned a law degree at the University of Montreal, a master's degree in political economy at Harvard University, and then studied politics in Paris from 1946–47, followed by an academic year at the London School of Economics from 1947–48.

After backpacking throughout Eastern Europe, the Middle East, and Far East, Pierre returned to Canada, where he worked in Ottawa as an advisor within the Canadian government. He then returned to Montreal, where he championed the rights of workers during the violent asbestos strike in Quebec.

Practicing law in Montreal, Pierre became an associate professor of law at the University of Montreal in 1961 and four years later won election to the House of Commons. From 1966–1967 he served as parliamentary secretary to Prime Minister Lester Pearson, who served as an informal mentor to Pierre. He continued in politics, reaching the office of prime minister in 1968, as Pearson resigned. His personality and style suited the times and by spring of 1968 a wave of "Trudeaumania" had swept Canada. Trudeau became a star. He appealed to all the demographics – young and old, French and English, east and west, and he was admired by male and female alike.

He backflipped into swimming pools, wore sandals in the House of Commons, hobnobbed with famous celebrities, and generally glamorized Canadian politics. He married a woman half his age in 1971. Six years and three children later, they were separated; they divorced in 1984. In 1990, Pierre was named the father of a girl born to a constitutional expert and longtime admirer. He was 71, she was 36.

Flamboyant, dashing, and daring, Pierre was also a man of substance, facilitating seminal changes that included the Official Languages Act, wage and price controls, the Canadian Charter of Rights and Freedoms, and the patriation of Canadian constitution. He also appointed the first woman governor-general in 1984.

Although he showed sympathy to the French-Canadian minority, as prime minister he continually advocated the principle of "one Canada," opposing Francophone separatism. He spoke from the beginning of creating a "just society" and a strong central government. In his first term, he established French as an official language, along with English. After 11 years in office, his Liberal government suffered a narrow defeat at the polls in 1979. The Progressive Conservative Party election victory was short-lived, however, and another election was called mere months later. On February 8, 1980, Pierre was once again returned to the office of prime minister, with a parliamentary majority.

Trudeaumania cooled in the 1980s and in 1984 Trudeau resigned from political office, taking himself out of the public eye. In 1998, he lost his youngest son Michel in an avalanche, which drew him closer to his other two sons. In 2000, a state funeral honored his life and achievements as the nation of Canada deeply mourned his death.

Words of Wisdom

I went home, discussed it with the boys, put them to bed. I walked until midnight in the storm, then I went home and took a sauna for an hour and a half. It was all clear. I listened to my heart and saw if there were any signs of my destiny in the sky – and there were none – there were just snowflakes.

Reason before passion.

Plato

c. 428–347 BCE

One of the most creative and important philosophers of the ancient world, Plato's work has had profound influence on Western thought.

Born of aristocratic parents in Athens, Greece, Plato had royal blood from a line of early Greek kings and he sought to combine his philosophical teachings with politics from the beginning. His schooling, writings, and life attest to a broader scope of thought, however. His influence on social ethics, religion, and the arts, as well as on politics, are only a few fields that bear Plato's philosophical stamp.

Plato's father died when Plato was a child and his mother remarried. He enjoyed a broad range of elementary studies, attending the gymnasium like most boys his age. The gymnasium contained a running track, jumping pits, javelin ranges, boxing rings, and ballgame arenas. He was a champion wrestler. Music and the letters were also part of his elementary education and his teachers often praised his love of hard work and study.

As a young man, Plato wrote poetry and painted. He probably entered a professional school, where he apprenticed in law under his stepfather. In his early years, he had political ambitions, but the corrupt political leadership of Athens dissuaded him from entering politics as a career. He was especially influenced by his master teacher, Socrates, who died at the hands of the Athenian government when he was about 30 years old. Fearing for his own safety and disillusioned by the Athenian democracy, Plato left Athens temporarily and traveled to Italy, Sicily, and Egypt. It was during his travels that he began writing his famous dialogues, seen by many scholars as memorials to the life and teaching of Socrates. The early dialogues focus on wisdom, with the main character, Plato, showing that the wise one is one who knows he does not know.

When he was in his early 40s, Plato founded the Academy in Athens, often described as the first European university. The school provided a comprehensive curriculum devoted to research and instruction in philosophy and the sciences. Most of Plato's later life was dedicated to teaching and guiding students in the activities of the Academy. Aristotle was the institution's most prominent student. After the founding of the Academy, Plato began writing the middle dialogues, widely considered his greatest work.

When he was in his 60s, Plato was invited to the Greek state of Syracuse to tutor a new ruler there. Having written *The Republic*, his famous dialogues about the philosopher-king, Plato went with high hopes of putting his thought into practice through the new head of state. His dreams were crushed, however, as the trip turned out to be a disaster. He returned from Syracuse and wrote the later dialogues, which more completely reflect Plato's own philosophical development. The ideas in the work are contributed to Plato himself, though Socrates continues to be the main character in many of the dialogues.

After one more failed trip to Syracuse, Plato returned to the Academy, where he spent his remaining years lecturing and writing.

Words of Wisdom

Thinking: The talking of the soul with itself.

The beginning is the most important part of the work.

Rhythm and harmony find their way into the inward places of the soul.

Pope John Paul II

1920 –

Pope John Paul II is the first non-Italian pope in nearly 500 years. He is known for his deep conservatism, ecological philosophies, and unprecedented international travel.

Pope John Paul II, born Karol Wojtyla in Wadowice, Poland, was a passionate, athletic young man who turned to the religious life by the time he was 22. Throughout his life, he has taken firm stands on controversial subjects such as birth control and the ecology, and he has traveled far and wide to expound upon God's love.

Karol's father was an officer in the Polish army and his mother was a former schoolteacher. He loved sports as a child, playing soccer as a goalie and taking daredevil swims in the Swaka River. He was an excellent student and served as class president. Growing older, he developed a love of theater and considered the life of an actor. For a while he pursued this vocation, along with the study of literature, while working as a stonecutter in a rock quarry. As a youth, Karol was active in a Christian democratic underground organization and he helped Jews find refuge from the Nazis.

While convalescing from an injury, he decided to join the priesthood and by 1946 he was ordained. For about 12 years, he was a university chaplain, teaching ethics at Krakow and Lublin. In 1958, he became auxiliary bishop of Krakow and four years later assumed leadership of the diocese and became a vicar. He was outspoken about communism and corrupt government officials.

From 1964, he rose quickly through the religious hierarchy of the Roman Catholic Church. In that year he became archbishop of Krakow, and in 1967, a cardinal. As a cardinal, he was an active participant in the Second Vatican Council, known for its many reforms, and between 1967–1977 he represented five international bishops' synods, starting a lifelong cycle of regular travel. He was elected pope on October 16, 1978.

Pope John Paul II is the first Polish pope and the first non-Italian pope since Pope Adrian VI in 1522. As pope, he continued the many travels he had begun as cardinal, visiting Africa, Asia, and the Americas in the 1980s and 1990s. In September 1993, he became the first pope to visit the Baltic republics. He facilitated the restoration of democracy and religious freedom throughout Eastern Europe, especially in his native Poland. He also dealt firmly with dissent within the church, reaffirming Roman Catholic teachings against abortion and artificial methods of human reproduction and birth control, as well as against homosexuality, while confirming the teaching of priestly celibacy. He has resolutely resisted secularization of the church, continuing to reject ordination of women and opposing political participation by priests.

In 2000, the Pope asked forgiveness for sins committed by Roman Catholics throughout history. Though he mentioned no specific incidents, many have assumed that the Crusades and the Inquisition, as well as inaction during the Holocaust, were the specific errors for which the church requested forgiveness.

In 1981, the Pope suffered severe wounds when he was shot as he entered St. Peter's Square to address a general audience. His hospital recovery lasted nearly three months, but he healed fully. Two days after Christmas in 1983, he visited his would-be assassin in prison, and has kept confidential their conversation.

Words of Wisdom

The search and discovery of God's will for you is a deep and fascinating endeavor.

Respect for life and for the dignity of the human person also extends to the rest of creation, which is called to join man in praising God.

Respect for life, and above all for the dignity of the human person, is the ultimate guiding norm for any economic, industrial, or scientific purpose.

Samuel Taylor Coleridge

1772–1834

Samuel Taylor Coleridge was an outstanding English poet, philosopher, and leader of the Romantic movement, in spite of a serious opium addiction.

Samuel Taylor Coleridge, nicknamed STC or Col, was the youngest of ten children, born in Ottery St. Mary, England, to clergyman John and his mother Ann Bowden. In spite of a painful illness that resulted in an opium addiction, he managed to write brilliant prose, poetry, and criticism, earning a measure of fame as leader of the Romantic Movement. He shared that spot with his cohort William Wordsworth, who eventually estranged himself from Col.

It is said that an early all-night escapade helped shape Col's mystical poetry. He ran away from home at the age of seven and the outdoor events of that night frequently showed up in the imagery of his poems, as well as in the notebooks he kept for most of his adult life.

When his father died, Col was nine years old and was sent away to a London charity school for children of the clergy. There he devoured books and excelled in his studies, earning first place in his class. His brother died when Col was 18 and his sister one year later. Because he experienced excruciating pain from severe rheumatism, Col began taking laudanum, which eventually resulted in a lifelong opium addiction, an addiction he was constantly trying to kick. He went to university from 1791 until 1794, where he absorbed political and theological ideas then considered radical, especially those of Unitarianism. When poetic fame eluded him, he joined the army, an act his brother George reversed by arranging his discharge by reason of insanity.

Shortly after his military dismissal, Col struck up a friendship with the intellectual Robert Southey. The two planned to form a utopian society in Pennsylvania, a plan they soon abandoned. The two men married sisters, and for Col the marriage proved an unhappy one.

In 1795, he met and began what was to be a lifelong friendship with the poet William Wordsworth and Wordsworth's sister Dorothy. The two men published a joint volume of poetry, *Lyrical Ballads*, that became a landmark in English poetry; it contained the first great works of the romantic school, such as the famous "The Rime of the Ancient Mariner."

Col moved to the Lake Country in 1800. He struggled financially and physically for many years, taking jobs as a journalist, lecturer, and literary critic. He continued to publish, and financial donations and grants supplemented his literary income.

Col became estranged from his family when his son Berkley died. Going into seclusion to avoid dealing with the intense pain this loss brought him, he didn't see his family for more than eight years. He took up residence in the home of James Gillman, a physician and admirer, in 1816, hoping that the doctor would help him kick his opium habit. The good doctor was unable to help Col with his addiction.

In spite of his addiction, his estrangement from his family, and his inability to achieve financial security, Col died peacefully, leaving only his books and manuscripts behind.

Words of Wisdom

Advice is like snow – the softer it falls, the longer it dwells upon, and the deeper it sinks into the mind.

Water, water everywhere,
And all the boards did shrink.
Water, water everywhere,
Nor any drop to drink.

To most men, experience is like the stern lights of a ship, which illumine only the track it has passed.

Shirley Temple Black

1928–

American motion-picture actress Shirley Temple Black was, in her youth, one of the most successful child stars in history.

Shirley Temple was born in Santa Monica, California, and was guided by an ambitious mother, who pushed her onto the motion picture stage at the age of three. As a child, she starred in more than 40 major motion pictures and 50 major television productions. As an adult, she has served as a U.S. delegate to the United Nations and to many international conferences and summits on cooperative treaties and the human environment.

At the age of five, *Stand Up and Cheer* propelled Shirley Temple to celebrity. Four movies followed that year. She became known for her blond mop of curls and her cute lisp, and for her talented singing and dancing. At the end of 1934, she received a special Academy Award for her contribution to film. She was six years old.

At the height of her career, from 1935 to 1938, Shirley was the biggest box-office attraction in Hollywood, and the revenues from her films helped make 20th Century Fox a major film studio. During the Great Depression of the 1930s, Shirley Temple was a ray of light. Adored by the public, she tap-danced and sang her way into the hearts of the America.

Shirley was also known for her professional approach to her work. During Wee Willie Winkie, the nine-year-old worked hard to impress director John Ford, who won her eternal love by treating her as a grownup, brushing off her attempts at girlish charm and childlike naiveté. She delighted in doing her own stunt work, typically working harder and longer than everyone else.

Time started catching up with the child star as she entered adolescence. After her Fox contract ended in 1940, she went on to make a few modest films that were box office failures. Nevertheless, her teen years were happy ones, filled with sodas, sock hops, and schoolwork. She bounced back from the loss of her screen appeal to live a happy, fulfilled life, retiring from Hollywood altogether in the late 1940s.

She ran for Congress unsuccessfully in 1967. Though she lost the election, she went on to display her trademark tenacity by taking on a long and successful career with the United Nations and the State Department. She was a member of the U.S. delegation to the United Nations from 1969–1970, ambassador to Ghana from 1974–1976, and became the first woman in U.S. history to serve as chief of protocol. She also served as ambassador to Czechoslovakia from 1989–1992, during the administration of President George Bush.

Though her diplomatic skills have kept her busy in the political arena, Shirley has also lent her expertise in the business sector, sitting on the corporate board of directors for such major companies as Del Monte, Bancal Tri-State, Fireman's Fund Insurance, and Walt Disney Productions.

She has raised three children and continues to lead an active life.

Words of Wisdom

You've got to S-M-I-L-E to be H-A-double P-Y!

Good luck needs no explanation.

Make-believe colors the past with innocent distortion, and it swirls ahead of us in a thousand ways – in science, in politics, in every bold intention. It is part of our collective lives, entwining our past and our future…a particularly rewarding aspect of life itself.

Sojourner Truth

1797–1883

A former slave, Sojourner Truth was one of the earliest and most passionate female abolitionists.

Sojourner Truth, born Isabella Baumfree, a slave in upstate New York, labored for a succession of five masters until July 4, 1827, when slavery was finally abolished in New York State. Throughout her entire life, she spoke and traveled widely on behalf of abolishing slavery.

Her first activist protest unfolded in a courtroom, where she demanded the return of her youngest son, Peter, who had been illegally sold away from her to a slave owner in Alabama. After winning the case, she moved to New York City, where she worked as a housekeeper and became deeply involved in religion. Soon after her emancipation, she had a vision that affected her profoundly, leading her – as she later described it – to develop a perfect trust in God and in prayer.

After 15 years in New York, she felt called to become a traveling preacher, taking the name Sojourner, or citizen of heaven and wanderer on earth, with the surname of Truth, on the grounds that God was her Father, and his name was Truth. She spoke at numerous church gatherings of both black and white congregations, quoting the Bible extensively from memory and speaking against slavery and for improved legal status for women. When she rose to speak, wrote one observer, "Her commanding figure and dignified manner hushed every trifler to silence." Audiences were often brought to tears by her touching stories.

After several months of traveling, friends encouraged Sojourner to go to the Northampton Association, which was founded in 1841 as a cooperative community dedicated to abolitionism, pacifism, equality, and the betterment of human life. When the association disbanded in 1846, she remained in Northampton, moving for the first time into her own home, with a loan from a friend. She never learned to read or write, but she dictated her memoirs to a secretary and they were published in 1850. Around this time she discovered the women's rights movement and added it to her list of causes. The book and her presence as a speaker made her a sought-after figure on the anti-slavery women's rights lecture circuit. She is particularly remembered for the famous "Ain't I a Woman?" speech delivered at the women's rights convention in Akron, Ohio, in 1851.

Sojourner moved to Michigan in 1857 and continued her advocacy. After the Emancipation Proclamation was issued, she moved to Washington, D.C., where in her late 60s she began working with former slaves. During the Civil

War, she had collected supplies for black volunteer regiments, and, in tribute to her efforts, she was received at the White House by President Lincoln in 1864. She was appointed to the National Freeman's Relief Association in 1864, where she worked diligently to better conditions for African-Americans.

She lived long enough to see her people receive freedom, but she never stopped her efforts to win more equality for them. Until her dying day, she continued to speak out for her race.

Words of Wisdom

Religion without humanity is poor human stuff.

Truth burns up error.

Those are the same stars, and that is the same moon, that look down upon your brothers and sisters, and which they see as they look up to them, though they are ever so far away from us, and from each other.

Vaclav Havel

1936–

With profound words and passionate conviction, Vaclav Havel helped topple a totalitarian regime.

A man of deep thought and meaningful action, Vaclav Havel moved beyond what were considered class and educational limitations to become a world-renowned playwright, as well as president of both Czechoslovakia and the Czech Republic.

Born and raised in Prague, he grew up in a well-known family of businessmen and intellectuals. His father was a building contractor; his uncle, owner of the country's main film studio. Because of his bourgeois background, Vaclav was unable to obtain a first-class education. His schooling consisted of evening classes at a college preparatory school, which he attended while working as a chemical laboratory technician during the day. After a compulsory, two-year stint in the military, he went to work at the Prague theater, drawn there by family tradition and his own interest in drama.

Vaclav's first plays were produced at the Prague theater in the 1960s, when the thaw in the political climate also allowed him to publish his essays. His best-known plays, *The Garden Party*, written in 1963, and *The Memorandum*, written in 1965, were humorous parables of life under Communism, winning international acclaim and focusing attention on sensitive political issues of the time. His plays greatly influenced the cultural awareness dawning on Czechoslovakia in the 1960s.

After Soviet troops invaded Czechoslovakia in 1968, Vaclav Havel formally denounced the Soviet Union, and his plays were subsequently banned in his country. In 1975, he wrote an open letter to Czechoslovakian President Husak, pointing out the injustices within Czechoslovak society. In 1977, he became an even louder voice with the publication of Charter 77, a document that helped shape the character of open dissent in Czechoslovakia. In 1979, he became a co-founder of the Committee for the Defense of the Unjustly Persecuted. As a result of his civil stance, he was imprisoned three times for a total of five years.

Vaclav continued to dissent, placing pressure on the totalitarian regime at a time when dialogue was beginning to emerge between the Soviet Union and the Western democracies. The Czechoslovak people increasingly expressed dissatisfaction with the country's leadership and were less and less willing to accept the repressive policies of the Communist regime. The pressure on Soviet rule continued to increase until the violent repression of a student demonstration in 1989, which sparked an explosion of civil unrest. Vaclav positioned himself at the forefront of this wave of protest, which culminated in the victory over Communist rule. In 1989, he was elected President of Czechoslovakia, promising to lead the country to free elections, which he did.

In the spring of 1992, economic disagreements led to new negotiations between the Czechs and the Slovaks, resulting in the decision to create two separate republics, the Czech Republic and Slovakia. Vaclav resigned as president of Czechoslovakia and was promptly elected president of the new Czech Republic in 1993.

Vaclav has remained a strong voice for unity, peace, and justice throughout his political career, promoting the formation of the European Union and leading the way to the Czech Republic's membership in an expanded NATO. He has received countless medals and citations for his profound and stirring literature, and for his astounding political accomplishments.

Words of Wisdom

Hope is a state of mind, not of the world. Hope, in this deep and powerful sense, is not the same as joy that things are going well, or willingness to invest in enterprises that are obviously heading for success, but rather an ability to work for something because it is good.

The salvation of this world lies nowhere else but in the human heart.

As soon as man began considering himself the source of the highest meaning in the world and the measure of everything, the world began to lose its human dimension, and man began to lose control of it.

For Your Own Inspirational Guide's Biography

NAME:

DATES:

Two-sentence description of the subject's life and accomplishments:

Subject's place of birth and early experiences that affected later life:

Most notable accomplishments:

Special challenges:

Of particular interest:

The subject will be most remembered for:

Words of Wisdom

Three quotes:

Bibliography

The following books helped inform my writing. Most of the quotations in this book came from the Internet and the websites listed below.

Anderson, Peggy, comp. *Great Quotations from Great Women*. Celebrating Excellence Publishing. 1992.

Chopra, Deepak. *Quantum Healing*. Bantam Books, 1990.

Covey, Stephen. et al. *First Things First: To Live, To Love, To Learn, To Leave a Legacy*. Fireside, 1996.

Donahugh, Donald L. *The Middle Years*. The Saunders Press, 1981.

Dowling, Colette. *Red Hot Mamas*. Bantam Books, 1996.

Encarta. Microsoft Corporation. 1993–2000.

Erik Erikson, H. *The Life Cycle Completed*. W. W. Norton & Company, 1998.

—. *Childhood and Society*. W. W. Norton & Company, 1993.

—. *Identity: Youth and Crisis*. W. W. Norton & Company, 1994.

Goldstein, Ross E. and Diana Landau. *Fortysomething*. Jeremy P. Tarcher, Inc., 1990.

Gorney, Sondra and Claire Cox. *After Forty*. The Dial Press, 1973.

Henderson, Sallirae. *A Life Complete*. Scribner, 2000.

Hyatt, Carole. *Shifting Gears*. Simon & Schuster, 1990.

Jung, Carl G. *The Collected Works of C. G. Jung*. trans. R. F. C. Hull. Princeton University Press, 1960.

Orman, Suze. *The 9 Steps to Financial Freedom*. Crown Publishers Inc., 1997.

Peck, M. Scott. *Further along the Road Less Traveled*. Touchstone Books, 1998.

Puner, Morton. *Getting the Most Out of Your Fifties*. Crown Publishers, 1977.

Robinson, John C. *Death of a Hero, Birth of a Soul: Answering the Call of Midlife*. Council Oak Distribution, 1997.

Sheehy, Gail. *Passages: Predictable Crises of Adult Life*. E. P. Dutton & Co., 1976.

—. *New Passages: Mapping Your Life Across Time*. Ballantine Books, 1995.

Shenk, David. *Data Smog: Surviving the Information Glut*. HarperEdge, 1997.

INTERNET SOURCES

www.quotationspage.com

www.famous-quotations.com

www.quoteland.com

www.arthistory.sbc.edu/sacredplaces.com

www.english.upenn.edu/~afilreis/88/dickinson-bio.html

info.greenwood.com/books/0313258/0313258481.html

www.wic.org/bio/roosevel.htm

www3.sympatico.ca/mcm.donovan/trudeau/quickbio.htm

www.clevernet.on.ca/pierre_trudeau

sc94.ameslab.gov/TOUR/alincoln.html

freepages.genealogy.rootsweb.com/~mtbagby/AbeLincolnBio.htm

womenshistory.about.com

www.anc.org.za/people

www.cmgww.com/music/

www.angelfire.com

www.ufw.org

www.usdreams.com/ChavezW37.html